STRONG & NORTHERN

THE HENDERSON'S RELISH COOK BOOK

STRONG & NORTHERN

ISBN: 9781910863527

Thank you to: The Freeman family, Matt Davies and all the staff at Henderson's Relish.

The chefs, staff and students at Sheffield College for the dishes; Andy Gabbitas, Joseph Hunt, Gregg Rodgers, James Rodgers, Steven Salt, Neil Taylor and Julie Travis.

Chef Adam Clark from Make No Bones for the Vegan recipes.

Written by: Katie Fisher

Food photography: Paul Cocker

Additional photography:
Marc Barker (www.marcabarker.co.uk)
Matt Crowder (www.mattcrowder.co.uk)
Ian M Spooner (www.ims-photography.co.uk)

Edited by: Phil Turner, Anna Tebble

Design: Paul Cocker

Contributors: Rupinder Casimir, Lydia Fitzsimons, Joseph Food, Nicholas Hallam, Michael Johnson, Sarah Koriba, Marek Nowicki, Paul Stimpson

Cover art: Matt Brewin (www.iamaretoucher.com)

Printed in Great Britain by Bell and Bain Ltd, Glasgow

me:ze
PUBLISHING

Published by Meze Publishing Limited
Unit 1b, 2 Kelham Square
Kelham Riverside
Sheffield S3 8SD
Web: www.mezepublishing.co.uk
Telephone: 0114 275 7709
Email: info@mezepublishing.co.uk

This book is dedicated to the city of Sheffield.

We would like to thank everyone who contributed their time
and amazing stories to be featured in this book.

FOREWORD

Hendersons (Sheffield) Ltd has been making Henderson's Relish since 1885. Now in our 135th year, we remain an independent, family-owned business and are still mixing, blending and bottling Sheffield's famous sauce to our secret recipe.

The Freeman family has owned Hendersons for three generations. They are extremely proud of Henderson's Relish, and the role it plays in the culinary and cultural life of the city.

But really, Henderson's Relish belongs to Sheffield. It's all of ours. Whether you've just arrived, have been here for years, or have never left, there's something about this city's spicy sauce that is different, just right. Find Henderson's Relish, and you'll find a home, right here.

The city of Sheffield is changing and growing. Our food reflects not only our history, but the influence of diverse cultures and the demands of modern lifestyles and dietary requirements. Yet Henderson's Relish remains and thrives.

There are over 60 recipes in this, our 'Strong & Northern' cook book. Traditional favourites rub along with new and different dishes that you can find across the city. Splash it on or stir it in; however you use Henderson's, there's something here for you.

But don't just take my word for it. Each recipe in this cook book features someone who loves Sheffield. Through their work, they serve us and the city. We're honoured to highlight their contributions as we celebrate Sheffield as it is today.

I hope you enjoy these latest Henderson's recipes.

Matt Davies – General Manager

CONTENTS

FANS OF HENDERSON'S RELISH

THE STORY OF HENDERSON'S RELISH

This 'Strong and Northern' Henderson's Relish cook book celebrates the great tradition of Sheffield's spicy sauce. The new collection of recipes showcases modern as well as traditional favourites, and highlights how Sheffield people have always used Henderson's Relish: splashing it over their favourite meals, whether that's a proper pie or Friday fish and chips.

In a city which has given the world so much in the form of manufacturing, music, film, art and sport, Henderson's Relish remains a source (or should that be sauce?) of great admiration for Sheffielders. It embodies the very essence of what makes the city great; the cultural lifeblood behind its character and surely its favourite table sauce.

The story of Henderson's Relish began in 1885, at the general store of Henry Henderson. In his occupation as a dry salter and wholesale chemist, he would blend ingredients to create various mixtures which he would then sell from his premises on Broad Lane. This pioneer first sold his creation from large wooden barrels that filled customers' glass bottles with a spicy sauce unlike any other, for just a penny apiece.

Henderson's Relish was a success from the beginning. He continued to sell barrel after barrel until 1910, the year in which a pickle manufacturing company called Shaws of Huddersfield saw enough potential to make Henderson an offer to purchase the business. The bid was accepted, and the company moved less than half a mile up the street to their second address and first factory at 66 Leavygreave Road.

George Shaw's daughter Miriam married a gentleman called Charles William Hinksman and in 1940, the company became limited in its own right as Hinksman bought the company from Shaws. It was during Mr Hinksman's tenure that the decision was made to move premises to the now iconic Sheffield address on Leavygreave Road, instantly recognisable as the old Henderson's factory.

Charles Hinksman later remarried Gladys Freeman, and following his death the company was given to her. It has remained in the hands of the Freeman family ever since. In 1991, ownership of the company was passed to Dr Kenneth Freeman, a retired GP who although not living in Sheffield, made weekly visits to mix the secret recipe.

During these years, Dr Freeman oversaw ground-breaking developments in the company's profile alongside his wife Pamela. Henderson's Relish was listed in only one local supermarket, the Co-op. Deliveries to local customers were made in an old Land Rover van; the boot stacked high with cases for the driver to unload at corner shops and independent retailers around the city.

Pamela and Dr Freeman began to visit various supermarket chains, carrying a bottle of Henderson's to tempt potential buyers. Their hard work eventually paid off and Sainsbury's became the company's largest supermarket partner in 1996. From that point on, the product started to sell itself as more local supermarkets came on board; Henderson's Relish became much more accessible for its adoring Sheffield audience and word spread further afield.

The success of Henderson's in its home town had previously been a rather modest, understated affair. Yet over the last decade, the Henderson's Relish brand has gained 'cult status' in the city. As a selection of famous fans such as Richard Hawley sing its praises, Sheffield locals continue to take pride in the iconic bottle with its orange label.

November 2013 marked the end of an era for Henderson's Relish as the company moved from the humble Leavygreave Road building, to new premises at Sheffield Parkway Business Park. It only helped the company continue to grow, and these days shops stocking Henderson's can be found as far away as Whitby, Filey, Scotland and even London!

Bottles of Henderson's Relish are dispatched around the world on a regular basis. While filming Sharpe in 2008, Sean Bean ordered a batch of Henderson's to his film set in India. In 2009, Dr Freeman sent litre bottles of Henderson's to troops serving in Afghanistan. And, in 2014, more giant bottles were sent out to a Sheffield soldier at the request of his wife, inadvertently converting an entire squadron into Henderson's addicts by doing so!

Customers in Singapore, Australia, the United States and even Hong Kong have all been in touch with the Henderson's Relish sales department. Families have been known to send bottles over to their kin living in New Zealand, Spain and Canada. It's fair to say that despite its local connotations, Henderson's Relish certainly gets around!

The newly-launched miniature bottle has been a popular addition to this growing trend. Starting life as 'Holiday Hendo's' – for Sheffielders to take away where their special sauce couldn't be found – the 31ml glass bottles are now an essential travel accessory and wedding favour. More recently, sachets of Henderson's have joined the range and an increasing online presence has allowed the company to send its famous product around the world at the click of a button.

Henderson's Relish remains an independent family business with deep roots and pride in the Sheffield community, which it has served for over a century. Its success has seen it become a Sheffield institution, adorning the kitchen tables and cupboard shelves of South Yorkshire families across the generations.

SHEFFIELD
OUR HOMETOWN

Hendersons has seen a lot of change over the years, from Sheffield's industrial heritage through to the creative and cultural rebirth our city is experiencing today. Just like us, Sheffield has never really shouted about all the exciting things that happen between its seven hills. As you flick through the pages in this book, you'll find people who are testament to that: we want to recognise and celebrate their contributions to the city and its unique, strong and northern character.

A long time before it was the trendy thing to do, Sheffield was supporting independent traders and craftspeople who worked for themselves and produced quality goods. These 'little mesters' made small tools and cutlery – such as knives forged from the infamous Sheffield steel – in rented workshops that formed the backbone of those industries. Their dedication and skill is reflected in the creative scene of the Steel City today which hosts and inspires an incredible range of talent.

Music is a huge part of this artistic flair and Hendersons has supported the many brilliant names to emerge from Sheffield over the years, including Richard Hawley and Artic Monkeys to name just a few. Limited edition bottles raise money for local charities, and celebrate events too, such as the tenth anniversary of Tramlines. The spirit of this annual music festival lives not just on its main stage, but in the bars and pubs across the city which have always hosted fringe performances, and it's in the city's network of working men's clubs where Sheffield talent has formed and forged.

No eatery is complete without a bottle of Henderson's Relish on the table, of course, and you'll find the city's cafés, pubs and restaurants all featuring the famous sauce. The food and drink on offer in Sheffield is improving and evolving, meeting the demands of modern day lifestyles and dietary requirements, and embracing growing trends such as veganism, while traditional favourites such as meat and potato pie remain as popular as ever.

This positive attitude towards diversity transcends what we eat and stands out as a foundation of the city's culture too. Sheffield was the first city in the UK to be designated a City of Sanctuary for asylum seekers and refugees, back in 2007. People here take pride in offering help and support to others no matter what their background, and this generosity can also be found in charitable and volunteer-run organisations from food banks to outreach centres for vulnerable people.

There's much to be proud of in Sheffield, not least its sporting prowess and a particular love for 'the beautiful game' which in fact originated here: one of the oldest recorded football matches took place at Bents Green in the 1790s. With a third of the city in the Peak District National Park, the natural beauty of our green spaces enable a whole range of active pursuits to flourish: mountain biking, bouldering, walking and fell running are as popular as indoor ice hockey and basketball. From boxing champions to gold medal winners, and with world class training centres at EIS, investing in sports is a tradition that Sheffield has nurtured for centuries.

Our nostalgia for the past helps Sheffield to preserve and celebrate its proud heritage, but we are not afraid to move forward and create something new either. Driven by people who contribute incredible things to this city every day, Sheffield continues to develop through difficult and changing times, always emerging stronger and more diverse on the other side. Hendersons is just one part of the fabric here, and we like to think it's synonymous with the deep attachment and appreciation people feel for Sheffield, because once you get to know it, you can't help but love it.

ABOUT
THIS BOOK

The idea behind this recipe collection is to celebrate the diversity and tradition of good food in Sheffield. From pork sancocho – a Caribbean stew featuring plantain and cassava – to fish and chips with mushy peas, these are hearty meals to feed you and your loved ones which can only be improved by an extra glug of Henderson's Relish at the table!

We've split them into seven sections that represent home cooking, whatever your tastes and dietary preferences: Strong & Northern, Family Favourites, One Pot Wonders, Pies & Pastries, Vegan Dishes, Cheese Dishes and Tasty Sides. Whether it's Sunday dinner for a crowd or a cosy supper on the sofa, you'll find old favourites and new ideas in this book to make the most of your favourite spicy sauce.

Fans of Hendo's have shared their thoughts on the Sheffield institution, as well as reflections about the city and personal connections to the various elements of its heritage and culture. Green spaces, iconic buildings, creative inspiration, charitable projects, fond food memories and the warmth of the people here are some favourite aspects of our unique city. Sheffield means something different to everyone but pride and affection for this place they call home, or that made such a strong impression in a short time, unites all these perspectives.

England footballer Millie Bright and former world squash champion Nick Matthew represent the city's sporting prowess, while renowned artist Joe Scarborough and inaugural poet laureate Otis Mensah are leading lights of Sheffield's thriving creative scene. Musicians, journalists, business owners, faith leaders, MPs, metal grinders and knife makers…all have contributed to the city in brilliant ways and have fascinating insights to share, not to mention a genuine love for Henderson's Relish and all the food you can splash it on or stir it in!

Photo: Paul Cocker

STRONG & NORTHERN

SHEFFIELD ASH

PREPARATION TIME: 15 MINUTES | COOKING TIME: 2 HOURS | SERVES: 6

1 onion
2 sticks of celery
150g carrots
150g potato
150g swede
600ml beef stock
30ml Henderson's Relish
1 tbsp vegetable oil
1 tbsp butter
850g stewing beef

First, prepare the vegetables. Peel and chop the onion, dice the sticks of celery after giving them a good wash, then peel and dice the carrots, potato and swede into pieces of roughly the same size. You may also want to add or substitute turnips, parsnips and other root veg.

Put all of the vegetables into a large pan with the stock and relish.

Cut the stewing beef into nice large chunks. You can use any cut that results in a lovely tender meat, including chuck, short rib with the bone in, oxtail or cross-cut shanks, but brisket and feather blade both work very nicely here.

Place a separate pan on a medium heat and fry the beef in the oil and butter until it is nicely browned. Add this to the pan of vegetables and stock, give everything a good stir and bring it up to the boil.

Turn the heat down and then simmer the ash for around 2 hours or until the beef is tender. Serve with dumplings, Yorkshire puddings, mashed potato or simply enjoy a big bowl on its own.

Photo: Leah Abdulla/Tim Cleasby Photography

As a child, on Thursdays my mum would routinely make us ash for tea. I never questioned why, it's just how it was. I'd go on to make it every Sunday for my son as a post-football treat. There are no airs and graces about it. I once went down to Castle Market to shop for a celebratory tea. The meat stall vendor asked, "what you making love?" "Beef bourguignon," I replied. He reacted pricelessly: "what, fancy stew?" Even when I moved to California for a few years, I'd receive Hendo's in the post wrapped in the Green 'Un. Long may it reign!

SAM PARSONAGE, BUSINESS OWNER

SHEFFIELD FISHCAKE

PREPARATION TIME: 45 MINUTES | COOKING TIME: 1 HOUR | SERVES: 8

FOR THE FISHCAKE

Vegetable oil
75g plain flour
½ tsp salt
125ml water
15ml malt vinegar
3-4 potatoes, peeled
Seasoned plain flour
500g cod or haddock, skinned and boned

FOR THE MUSHY PEAS

225g dried marrowfat peas
2 tbsp baking soda
Salt and pepper, to taste

FOR THE FISHCAKE

Preheat a deep fat fryer or a pan of vegetable oil to about 180°c.

Put the flour and salt into a bowl, add the water and vinegar then whisk until smooth.

Cut the potatoes into about 5mm thick slices. Trim the fish to pieces of about the same size. It needs to fit in between two pieces of potato to make a sandwich. Dip all the fish into the seasoned flour and shake off the excess.

Place the fish between two pieces of potato, dip the 'sandwich' into the batter and then lower it carefully into the hot oil. These fishcakes usually drop to the bottom, so be careful if you have a basket because the batter can get stuck in it.

Make a few more and drop them in as well. After 3 to 4 minutes they should be floating. Flip each fishcake over and cook on the other side for about the same amount of time.

Remove from the fryer and drain on kitchen paper before serving.

FOR THE MUSHY PEAS

Place the peas in a large bowl or stockpot; the peas will swell and need plenty of room to expand. Add the baking soda, cover with 285ml boiling water and stir to make sure the baking soda has dissolved. Leave the peas to soak overnight or for a minimum of 12 hours.

Drain the peas in a colander, and then place them in a large saucepan. Cover them with cold water and bring this to the boil. Lower the heat and simmer for approximately 30 minutes or until the peas have softened and turned mushy.

Season with salt and pepper then splash with Henderson's Relish to your own preference.

For me it's about sticking to my roots. I've been a keen Wednesday supporter since 1969 (who keeps going back for more punishment) but as a true Sheffielder, my proudest achievement is being part of the management team at Atkinsons, an institution that has been part of the city's fabric for many years.

DAVID CARTWRIGHT, ATKINSONS

DERBYSHIRE BREAKFAST

PREPARATION TIME: 5 MINUTES | COOKING TIME: 20 MINUTES | SERVES: 2

Drizzle of light olive oil

2 sausages

2 rashers of bacon

2 flat mushrooms

2 vines of cherry tomatoes

2 thick slices of black pudding

2 oatcakes (you can buy these in the supermarket)

FOR THE POACHED EGGS

1 tbsp white wine vinegar

2 free-range eggs

Salt and freshly ground black pepper

First, heat a flat grill plate (or griddle pan) over a low heat. Brush sparingly with light olive oil. Cook the sausages slowly on the hot plate for about 10 minutes, turning occasionally. Increase the heat to medium to cook the other ingredients as well, until the sausages have had about 20 minutes in total and are golden. Keep them hot on a plate in the oven if needed.

Snip a few small cuts into the fatty edge of the bacon. Place the bacon straight on to the grill plate and fry for 2 to 4 minutes on each side or until it is your preferred level of crispiness. The cooked bacon can be kept hot on a plate in the oven.

Brush away any dirt from the mushrooms and trim the stalk level with the mushroom top. Season with salt and pepper and drizzle over a little olive oil. Place stalk-side up on the grill plate and cook for 1 to 2 minutes before turning and cooking for a further 3 to 4 minutes. Avoid moving the mushrooms too much while cooking, as this releases the natural juices, making them soggy.

Drizzle the cherry tomatoes with a little olive oil. Place on the grill plate and cook them without moving for 2 minutes. Gently turn over and season again. Cook for a further 2 to 3 minutes until they are tender but still hold their shape.

Place the slices of black pudding on the grill plate and cook for up to 2 minutes on each side until slightly crispy.

Warm the oatcake through in the oven for about 2 minutes while you cook the poached eggs.

Fill a small pan just over a third full with cold water and bring it to the boil. Add the vinegar and turn it down to simmer.

Crack the eggs one at a time into a small bowl or cup and gently tip into the simmering water. Lightly poach them for 2 to 3 minutes. Remove with a slotted spoon and drain on kitchen towels. Season with salt and freshly ground black pepper. Serve immediately with the cooked breakfast.

Being a Southerner, I've been told many times I did the right thing by making Sheffield my home. As a passionate foodie, it didn't take me long to discover some of the treats Sheffield does best – pie and peas or a hot pork butty – all served with lots of Hendo's Relish! However, it took a honeymoon trip to Bakewell with my new wife Liz for us both to fall head over heels in love with the Derbyshire Oatcake.
Much more than a pancake, and simply better than toast, it was a food epiphany!

GARETH ROBERTS, REGATHER

BUBBLE 'N' SQUEAK

PREPARATION TIME: 10 MINUTES | COOKING TIME: APPROX. 30 MINUTES | SERVES: 4 (AS A SIDE)

FOR THE MASHED POTATO

500g floury potatoes (such as King Edward or Maris Piper)

50ml double cream

75g butter

Salt and pepper

FOR THE BUBBLE 'N' SQUEAK

100g butter or dripping, plus extra for brushing over the top

1 large onion, finely diced

200g cooked cabbage

500g mashed potato

Salt and pepper

FOR THE MASHED POTATO

Bring a large saucepan of water to the boil while you peel and chop the potatoes into evenly sized pieces. Put the potatoes into the pan and boil for about 15 minutes, or until tender. Transfer to a colander and drain well, then place back in the pan off the heat.

Heat the cream and butter in a small pan, then pour over the potatoes. Mash the potatoes using an electric hand whisk or potato masher until smooth and free from lumps. Season with pepper and a pinch of salt.

FOR THE BUBBLE 'N' SQUEAK

Melt half of the fat in a large frying pan. Add the onion and fry until soft and starting to turn golden, then add the cabbage and warm through.

Mix the cabbage and onion with the mashed potato and season well.

Melt the rest of the fat in the same pan. When bubbling, swirl around the pan and transfer the mash and cabbage mix into the pan. Level it out and push it into the corners.

Brush the top of the bubble and squeak with the additional melted butter or dripping and place into a hot oven at approximately 200°c and cook until the top is golden and crisp.

Turn the bubble 'n' squeak out onto a plate and cut into wedges. Serve with gravy or stew and plenty of Henderson's Relish on the table so everyone can splash some on.

I've seen a lot of change during my time in Sheffield — more in the last five years than over the previous 40 — including a renaissance in the specialised steel industry. We are still at the forefront of this new era, and The Steel Man project aims to recognise and celebrate that.

STEVE MEHDI, SCULPTOR

HOT ROAST PORK SANDWICHES

PREPARATION TIME: 5 MINUTES | COOKING TIME: 3 HOURS | SERVES: 8

FOR THE ROAST PORK

1.3kg pork belly
15g fennel seeds
Sea salt
100ml olive oil
2 carrots, chopped
2 sticks of celery, chopped
6 cloves of garlic, peeled and chopped
2 onions, chopped
½ bunch of fresh thyme
500ml white wine

FOR THE STUFFING

1 onion, peeled and finely chopped
1 tbsp vegetable oil
1 tbsp fresh sage, finely chopped
80g fresh white breadcrumbs
Salt and pepper
1 egg, beaten

TO SERVE

8 floury baps
Jar of apple sauce

FOR THE ROAST PORK

Preheat the oven to its highest temperature.

Using a sharp knife, score the skin down to the meat (try not to cut the meat), making the cuts very close together. Bash the fennel seeds and a good pinch of sea salt into a powder. Drizzle the oil over the scored skin, then sprinkle over the fennel and salt mixture, and rub all over so that everything gets into the scores and down into the meat.

Put the vegetables in a roasting tin with the thyme. Place the seasoned pork belly on top of the vegetables in the tray, and roast it for 10 to 15 minutes, or until the skin starts to bubble and turn golden brown.

Reduce the oven temperature to 170°c and roast for a further 1 hour 30 minutes. Finally, add the wine and cook for a further hour.

FOR THE STUFFING

Heat a small frying pan and sweat the onion in the oil until soft but not coloured. Mix together the onion, sage and breadcrumbs and season well.

Add enough of the beaten egg to bind the mixture together and then roll into individual balls. Place the stuffing balls in a roasting tin and cook in the oven for 30 minutes while the pork is roasting.

TO SERVE

Slice the pork belly and crackling, put it into baps with a few stuffing balls each and serve with apple sauce and Henderson's Relish.

I've lived in Sheffield since 1985 and my latest novel is set here, so the city still plays a big part in my life. I especially enjoy walking in the Peak District at weekends, where my favourite pub lunch is a hot pork sandwich with stuffing and a splash of Henderson's Relish.

MARINA LEWYCKA, AUTHOR

FISH AND CHIPS

PREPARATION TIME: 10 MINUTES | COOKING TIME: 10 MINUTES | SERVES: 4

FOR THE FISH

1 egg
250ml water
200g flour, plus 20g for dusting
Pinch of salt
Vegetable oil, for deep frying
4 fillets of haddock (200g each)

FOR THE CHIPS

1kg chipping potatoes

FOR THE MUSHY PEAS

225g dried marrowfat peas
2 tbsp baking soda
Salt and pepper, to taste

FOR THE FISH

Whisk the egg and water together then pour the mixture into the flour. Add a pinch of salt and whisk to form a batter.

Heat a deep fat fryer or pan of oil to 175°c.

Coat the fish in seasoned flour, then dip each piece into the batter. Gently lower the fillets into the hot oil and deep fry for 4 to 5 minutes until the batter is crisp and golden brown. Remove and drain on kitchen paper.

FOR THE CHIPS

Peel the potatoes and cut them into chips. Wash them well and dry them in a clean cloth. Cook the chips in a deep fat fryer at 165°c for about 5 minutes or until they are cooked. Drain them on kitchen paper, then refry the chips in hot oil at 185°c until they are golden brown. Drain them well and season with salt, then serve with the battered fish.

FOR THE MUSHY PEAS

Place the peas in a large bowl or stockpot; the peas will swell and need plenty of room to expand. Add the baking soda, cover with 285ml boiling water and stir to make sure the baking soda has dissolved. Leave the peas to soak overnight or for a minimum of 12 hours.

Drain the peas in a colander, and then place them in a large saucepan. Cover them with cold water and bring this to the boil. Lower the heat and simmer for approximately 30 minutes or until the peas have softened and turned mushy.

TO SERVE

Season with salt and pepper then splash with Henderson's Relish to your own preference.

I got into squash in Sheffield and it's taken me all around the world, but over my 20 year career the best thing was always the infrastructure, support and facilities that exist in our city. That meant I could still call Sheffield home, and return after each bout of travelling to recover with Sunday lunch at my mum's or dinner in a cosy pub! Having a good hearty meal seemed to reset me internally; it was my treat at the end of a training week so I could keep going, fuelled by a brilliant roast or proper fish and chips.

NICK MATTHEW, FORMER PROFESSIONAL SQUASH PLAYER

MINCE AND PANCAKES

PREPARATION TIME: 40 MINUTES | COOKING TIME: 35-40 MINUTES | SERVES: 6

FOR THE MINCE

1 tbsp oil

1 onion, chopped

500g lean minced beef

100g plain flour

30g tomato purée

1 dessertspoon Henderson's Relish

Salt and pepper

600ml beef stock

FOR THE PANCAKES

240g plain flour

Pinch of salt

565ml milk

2 eggs, beaten

30g butter, melted

Vegetable oil

FOR THE MINCE

In a large frying pan, heat the oil and add the onion. Cook until soft, then add the minced beef to the pan and cook until browned. Add the flour and tomato purée, mix well, then add the relish, season with salt and pepper and stir everything in. Slowly add the beef stock to the pan then simmer for about 20 minutes.

FOR THE PANCAKES

Sift the flour and salt into a bowl. Add the milk and eggs then whisk until smooth. Whisk in the melted butter then allow the batter to rest for 1 hour.

Heat a frying pan and add a little vegetable oil to it. Pour a small ladleful of batter into the centre of the pan, lift the pan and move it around to coat the base with batter. Put the pan back onto the heat and cook the batter on the first side until there is no liquid. Turn the pancake over and cook again until light golden brown. Repeat with the remaining batter, then serve with the mince.

Having been born in Barnsley, I'm an 'incomer' and so Henderson's Relish was part of my 'induction to Sheffield'. My husband (and business partner) Andy Hanselman and myself are both firm fans, which is probably just as well as we look out daily onto their business premises from our offices! It comes everywhere with us; friends in the US, South Africa and Italy have all been lucky recipients. Hendo's is also a standard ingredient in our 'Welcome to Sheffield' pack for friends and clients. From Aberdeen to Bournemouth, they're all sold!

JILL WHITE, ANDY HANSELMAN CONSULTING

BARNSLEY CHOPS

2 Barnsley chops
Salt and pepper
Olive oil
125ml red wine
2 tsp redcurrant jelly
300ml chicken stock
Splash of Henderson's Relish

Get a frying pan on a very high heat while you season the lamb chops generously with salt and pepper, then rub them with olive oil.

Place the lamb fat-side-down in the hot pan, and leave for a couple of minutes until crisp. Turn the heat down to medium, flip the chops over and cook for 5 minutes. Flip again and cook on the other side for 7 to 10 minutes. This will vary greatly from chop to chop. If you want to be completely accurate, cook the chops until the internal temperature reaches 60°c for rare or 65°c for medium. Use a probe to check this.

When they are done, rest the lamb chops on a warm plate or board while you make the sauce.

Turn the heat back up and add the red wine to the pan. Use this to pick up all the crusty bits on the bottom of the pan, scraping with a wooden spoon to deglaze the base. Stir in the redcurrant jelly, stock and Henderson's Relish then let the sauce bubble furiously until syrupy.

Check it for seasoning and when you're happy, pour the sauce over the lamb and serve with greens and mashed potato, or your favourite side.

The Sheffield Churches Soup Kitchen has been active now for over 32 years. We directly help out on the streets, providing hot drinks, food, bedding and clothing. We even cook a big communal Christmas dinner for around 100 vulnerable people. As its founder, I'm proud to see campaigns like Help Us Help starting to unify and organise separate charities together with city services and the public sector. The aim is to educate people about the complex issues the homeless deal.
Now more than ever there's an interlinked, diverse team all pushing to really improve their lives. I'm proud of the city's sense of direction.

BOBBIE WALKER, SOUP KITCHEN COORDINATOR

SHEPHERD'S PIE

PREPARATION TIME: 20 MINUTES | COOKING TIME: 1 HOUR | SERVES: 6

FOR THE MINCE

25g oil

1 large onion, finely chopped

500g minced lamb

15g plain flour

2 bay leaves

2 sprigs of fresh thyme

400g tinned chopped tomatoes

50g frozen peas

2 tsp Henderson's Relish

450ml lamb stock

Salt and pepper

FOR THE MASH

700g potatoes, peeled and quartered

75g butter

55ml milk

1 egg yolk

FOR THE MINCE

Heat the oil in a pan and sauté the onions for about 5 minutes, or until soft. Add the mince and fry until brown, breaking up any lumps with the back of a spoon. Stir in the flour then add the bay leaves, thyme, chopped tomato, peas and relish.

Mix everything well then add the stock. Bring to the boil, season and simmer for about 40 minutes, stirring regularly.

FOR THE MASH

Meanwhile, preheat the oven to 180°c and boil the potatoes in salted water until tender. Drain them well, then add the butter, milk and egg yolk. Mash until smooth and season to taste.

TO ASSEMBLE

Pour the meat into a casserole dish, pipe or spoon the mash over the top, then place the shepherd's pie in the oven to cook until the mash is golden brown.

I've been in the barbering industry for over 30 years, and almost all that time has been spent in Sheffield. Between teaching all over the world, coming home reminds me why I set up and stayed here; it's kind of a big village where everybody knows everybody and it feels so laid back compared to bigger cities.

JOTH DAVIES, BARBER

FISH PIE

PREPARATION TIME: 1 HOUR 30 MINUTES | COOKING TIME: 30-40 MINUTES | SERVES: 2

475ml whole milk

1 bay leaf

150g salmon fillet

100g undyed smoked haddock

100g coley fillet

15g butter

15g plain flour

50g grated cheddar

Salt and pepper

3 sprigs of dill or parsley

Small pinch of grated nutmeg

10 large prawns, cooked and peeled

100g mussels, cooked

FOR THE MASHED POTATO

500g floury potatoes (such as King Edward or Maris Piper)

100ml double cream

150g butter

Salt and pepper

Place the milk into a large saucepan and add the bay leaf, bring up to a simmer and then leave to infuse for 5 minutes. Meanwhile, check over the fish for bones, removing any that you find.

Once the milk has infused, add the coley and poach gently for 3 to 4 minutes. Remove carefully with a slotted spoon and set aside to cool. Repeat this with the salmon and then lastly the smoked haddock.

While the fish is cooling, make a roux. Melt the butter in a medium-sized pan. Once it's bubbling add the flour and beat it into the butter to form a roux. Cook for a few minutes, stirring regularly, then remove from the heat. Add a small amount of the hot milk and stir it into the roux really well. Add a little more milk and then place the pan back on the heat, stirring continually and adding the milk until you have a smooth sauce.

Allow the sauce to bubble for a few minutes, still stirring, until it thickens enough to coat the back of a spoon. Remove the sauce from the heat and add the cheese. Stir until melted and check for seasoning; it will need some pepper and, depending on the smoked haddock, it may need salt. Chop the dill or parsley and stir into the sauce along with the nutmeg, then set aside to cool.

Flake the poached fish into large chunks and remove all the skin. Place the fish, prawns and mussels into a pie dish, approximately 10 by 15cm. Pour over the sauce and gently stir through. Pipe the mashed potato over the fish mix, then either cook straight away or chill until needed.

When you are ready to cook the pie, preheat the oven to 200°c and place the pie on a tray to catch any drips. Bake for 30 to 40 minutes until the mashed potato is golden and the filling is bubbling and piping hot. Serve with fresh vegetables and a bottle of Henderson's Relish.

FOR THE MASHED POTATO

Bring a large saucepan of water to the boil while you peel and chop the potatoes into evenly sized pieces. Put the potatoes into the pan and boil for about 15 minutes, or until tender. Transfer to a colander and drain well, then place back in the pan off the heat. Heat the cream and butter in a small pan, then pour over the potatoes. Mash the potatoes using an electric hand whisk or potato masher until smooth and free from lumps. Season with pepper and a pinch of salt.

My family moved to Sheffield from Jamaica in the 60s, so my mum's cooking used spices and ingredients you wouldn't find in many English dishes. When we were kids, we didn't always appreciate these 'different' meals, and would ask for chips instead of rice! She got a job in the canteen at the Northern General and started to try other styles of food, which is where her first fish pie recipe came from. I've created my own version over the years, tailored to my palate for well-seasoned food, which is definitely thanks to my mum's wonderful cooking.

PAULETTE EDWARDS, RADIO PRESENTER

STEAK AND CHIPS

PREPARATION TIME: 5 MINUTES | COOKING TIME: 4-8 MINUTES, PLUS 4 MINUTES RESTING | SERVES: 4

FOR THE STEAK

4 x 200g sirloin steaks
Vegetable oil
Salt and pepper

FOR THE CHIPS

1kg chipping potatoes

FOR THE STEAK

Cut small slits across the line of fat on the steaks and drizzle a little oil over the fat. Heat a griddle pan over a high heat. Salt the edge of the fat on the steaks and place them onto the pan, standing them up on the fatty edge. Hold them there for a few seconds until the fat begins to run down the grooves of the pan; this is all the lubrication you will need to cook the steak.

Allow the steaks to fall over, season very lightly with salt and plenty of pepper, then grill for 2 minutes on each side for a rare steak; 3 minutes for medium; and 4 minutes for well done. However, remember the thinner the steak, the less the cooking time.

Once cooked, leave the steaks to rest on a warm plate in a warm place (such as a very low oven) for a few minutes, so that the juices will settle evenly within the meat, while also allowing the meat to relax and become even tenderer.

FOR THE CHIPS

Peel the potatoes and cut them into chips. Wash them well and dry them in a clean cloth. Cook the chips in a deep fat fryer at 165°c for about 5 minutes or until cooked.

Drain the chips on kitchen paper and then refry them in hot oil at 185°c until golden brown. Drain the chips, season them well with salt then serve with the steaks and Henderson's Relish for splashing over the lot.

Photo: Darren O'Brien/Guzelian

I'm a real simple food type of guy, so when it comes to home cooking, especially in winter, I like to make stews. I was born and bred on Hendo's so it's always been a go-to. Like our green open spaces, it's just part and parcel of the Sheffield way of life. Unless you walk into somewhere like a proper pie and mash shop you're just not going to see it. It's as humble as the rest of us but let's be honest, it's far better than any other sauce isn't it?

ANDREW VICKERS, STONEFACE CREATIVE

YORKSHIRE PUDDINGS & GRAVY

PREPARATION TIME: 30 MINUTES | COOKING TIME: 1 HOUR | MAKES: 8 LARGE OR 16 SMALL PUDDINGS

FOR THE PUDDINGS

Sunflower oil

140g plain flour

4 eggs

200ml milk

FOR THE ONION GRAVY

2 onions, sliced

1 tbsp vegetable oil

1 tbsp sugar

1 tbsp tomato purée

1 tbsp Henderson's Relish

1 tbsp gravy browning or soy sauce

250ml beef or vegetable stock

150ml dark ale or beer

FOR THE PUDDINGS

Preheat the oven to 230°c (fan 210°c) and pour a little sunflower oil evenly into two four-hole Yorkshire pudding tins, or two twelve-hole non-stick muffin tins. Place the tins in the oven to heat through for 10 to 15 minutes.

To make the batter, put the plain flour into a bowl and beat in the eggs until smooth. Gradually add the milk and continue beating until the mixture is completely free from lumps. Season the batter with salt and pepper then pour it into a jug.

Remove the hot tins from the oven. Carefully and evenly pour the batter into the holes. Place the tins straight back in the oven and leave undisturbed for 20 to 25 minutes until the puddings have puffed up and browned evenly. Serve immediately.

FOR THE ONION GRAVY

Fry the onions in the oil until soft and slightly golden around the edges. Add the sugar and tomato purée, cook through, then add the Henderson's, gravy browning or soy sauce, stock and ale. Bring to boil then reduce the heat and simmer for 25 minutes. The gravy should be slightly thick but not gloopy.

Photo: Georgina Martin

I've lived in Sheffield for my entire 81 years and like to stay local with my art. I'm drawn by the stories behind the scenes I'm looking at, because those stories are what join us together. Hendo's is a great example of this: something we all share in 'our native village' which is what I call Sheffield. Talk about one and you'll talk about the other: Hendo's is Sheffield. When you give something a nickname and it sticks, that's affection, and it should be savoured just like a bottle of the good stuff. Splash a bit in your Yorkshire pudding batter, on pies, any piece of meat – they're nothing without it.

JOE SCARBOROUGH, ARTIST

FAMILY FAVOURITES

CHICKEN CURRY

PREPARATION TIME: 15 MINUTES, PLUS 1 HOUR MARINATING | COOKING TIME: APPROX. 40 MINUTES | SERVES: 6

454g yoghurt
2 tsp salt
30g dried methi
100g butter, cubed
1 kg chicken thigh, diced
500g onion
10 cloves of garlic
4 red chillies
100g butter
1 tbsp olive oil
2 tsp coriander seeds
½ cinnamon stick
10 curry leaves
10 green cardamom pods
1 tsp turmeric powder
1 tsp chilli powder
1 tbsp cumin seeds
2 tbsp garam masala
5 black peppercorns
100g tinned chopped tomatoes
200g potatoes, diced
2 whole dried chillies, chopped
125ml red wine
Knob of fresh ginger, finely sliced
Good handful of fresh coriander

Stir the yoghurt, salt, methi and butter together then coat the diced chicken in the mixture and leave to marinate for 1 hour. Meanwhile, grind the onion, garlic and red chillies to a paste with a pestle and mortar, or using a food processor.

Transfer the chicken and marinade into a pan on a low heat. Cover with a lid and cook for 10 minutes. At the same time in a separate pan, fry the onion paste in the butter and olive oil. Add the coriander seeds, cinnamon stick, curry leaves, cardamom pods, turmeric, chilli powder, cumin seeds, garam masala and peppercorns, then cook for 30 minutes.

Add the chopped tomatoes to the spice mix and cook for a further 5 minutes. Using another pan, fry the potatoes and dried chillies in a little butter for 10 minutes, until the potatoes are golden.

Add the spiced tomato sauce and the fried potatoes to the pan with the chicken, cook until the meat is tender then add the red wine.

Fry the sliced ginger in a little butter until soft, then scatter this and the fresh coriander over the curry to serve, with Hendo's on the table for the finishing touch.

Sheffield is the most friendly and welcoming city in the UK – the 'big village'. This is the most important reason why I brought up my mixed heritage family here. Sheffield has always had an independent spirit and this shines though in the companies that are based here, and there is no better place to have built my own business. My wife is half Bengali, her dad has taught her to make a great curry and we create a great 'fusion' dish with a splash of Henderson's because there are very few things Hendo's can't improve. This mixture of South Yorkshire and Indian reflects our family; it's the best of two great cultures.

MARK HERBERT, WARP FILMS

LASAGNE AL FORNO

PREPARATION TIME: 25 MINUTES | COOKING TIME: 1 HOUR 20 MINUTES | SERVES: 2

1 pack of readymade lasagne sheets

FOR THE BOLOGNESE

½ onion

1-2 cloves of garlic

50g carrot

50g celery

200g minced beef

Splash of oil

Salt and pepper

¼ tsp dried oregano

½ tin of tomatoes

Generous splash of Henderson's Relish

FOR THE BÉCHAMEL

500ml milk

50g butter

50g flour

1 tsp mustard

100g cheese, grated

Salt and pepper

FOR THE BOLOGNESE

Finely dice the onion, garlic, carrot and celery. Seal the mince in a hot pan with a little oil. Remove the mince and add the chopped vegetables with a little more oil if needed. When they have softened, add the mince back to the pan, season to taste and stir in the oregano. Cook for a couple more minutes then add the tomatoes and however much Henderson's Relish you feel like. Leave the sauce to simmer for 30 minutes.

FOR THE BÉCHAMEL

Heat the milk gently without allowing it to boil. Melt the butter in a separate saucepan, then stir in the flour. Cook until the mixture looks drier and sandy. Slowly add some of the heated milk and whisk or beat with a wooden spoon until you have a smooth paste. Keep adding milk and mixing thoroughly, making sure there are no lumps, until all the milk is incorporated. Take the pan off the heat, add the mustard and cheese – keeping some back for the top – then season to taste. Make sure all the cheese has melted and the sauce is smooth.

TO ASSEMBLE

Spoon a layer of béchamel sauce into the lasagne dish. Place a layer of lasagne sheets over the top, then a layer of Bolognese sauce. Do another layer of pasta, then more Bolognese, then pasta, then a final layer of béchamel. Sprinkle the remaining grated cheese over the top and bake the lasagne at 180°c for 30 minutes or until bubbling and golden, then serve.

As an immigrant from down south I came late to Henderson's, having been brought up with a different geographically-specific sauce that will remain nameless. On moving to Sheffield 15 years ago I quickly saw the error of my ways, and I have been attempting to make up for lost time ever since in my consumption of Henderson's with as many food stuffs as possible. As a musician I spend a lot of time on the road eating bland food so the mini bottles of HR have been a particular godsend.

JON BODEN, FOLK MUSICIAN

CHILLI CON CARNE

PREPARATION TIME: 15 MINUTES | COOKING TIME: 40 MINUTES | SERVES: 4

1 tbsp oil

1 large onion, diced

2 cloves of garlic, crushed

1 red pepper, diced

1 heaped tsp hot chilli powder (or 1 level tbsp mild chilli powder)

1 tsp paprika

1 tsp ground cumin

500g lean minced beef

300ml beef stock

50ml Henderson's Relish

400g tinned tomatoes

½ tsp dried marjoram

1 tsp sugar

Salt and pepper

30g tomato purée

410g tinned red kidney beans

Put the pan over a medium heat, add the oil and leave it for 1 to 2 minutes until hot. Add the onion and cook, stirring fairly frequently, for about 5 minutes, or until the onion is soft. Add the garlic, red pepper, chilli powder, paprika and ground cumin. Give it a good stir, then leave it to cook for another 5 minutes, stirring occasionally.

Turn the heat up a bit, add the meat to the pan and break it up with your spoon or spatula. The mix should sizzle a bit when you add the mince. Keep stirring for at least 5 minutes, until all the mince is in uniform lumps and there are no more pink bits. Make sure you keep the pan hot enough for the meat to fry and become brown, rather than just stew. Add the beef stock to the mince along with the relish, tinned tomatoes, dried marjoram, sugar and a good shake of salt and pepper. Add the tomato purée and stir the sauce well.

Bring the whole thing to the boil, give it a good stir then put a lid on the pan. Turn down the heat until it is gently bubbling and leave for 20 minutes. Check on the chilli occasionally to stir it and make sure the sauce doesn't catch on the bottom of the pan or dry out. If it does, add a couple of tablespoons of water and make sure that the heat is low enough. Add the kidney beans and cook for 5 more minutes. Serve with soured cream and boiled long grain rice.

Henderson's is one of my 'magic ingredients', versatile and a must in all my slow-cooked dishes. It gives great depth of flavour to the sauce or jus in stews, casseroles, Bolognese and of course, our household favourite, chilli con carne, with extra chilli just for me! I have worked around the corner from the original Henderson's building for all my life, so how could I choose anything else?

CRISTIAN SINCLAIR, SINCLAIRS

HENDERSON'S BURGER

PREPARATION TIME: 5 MINUTES | COOKING TIME: 8 MINUTES | SERVES: 2

FOR THE HENDO'S CARAMELISED ONIONS

2 large white onions

3 tbsp unsalted butter

1 tbsp fine brown sugar

2 tbsp Henderson's Relish

Salt and pepper

FOR THE BURGER

400g good quality minced beef

100g onion, finely chopped

1 tsp tomato ketchup

1 tsp English mustard

1 tsp Henderson's Relish

1 tsp dried mixed herbs

Salt, to taste

TO SERVE

2 burger buns

Vine tomatoes, sliced

Rocket or other salad leaves

FOR THE HENDO'S CARAMELISED ONIONS

Peel and halve the onions before thinly slicing them. Add the butter to a large pan, and when melted add the onions. Sauté until soft, then add the sugar and Henderson's Relish. Cook for a further 30 to 40 minutes, stirring occasionally until the onions are a dark brown colour and have a slightly jammy texture. Season to taste with salt and black pepper, then cover and keep warm until needed.

FOR THE BURGER

Heat a little oil in a frying pan over a medium heat, then sauté the chopped onion until softened. Put this into a bowl with all the other ingredients and mix to combine. Using your hands might be easiest for this. Divide the mixture in half and shape the pieces to form two patties.

Fry the burger patties in the same pan over a medium heat with a little oil for 3 minutes on each side, or until cooked to your preference.

TO SERVE

Serve the burgers topped with Hendo's caramelised onions in the buns with accompaniments of your choice. We've added sliced vine tomatoes and fresh rocket with extra onion rings.

I've lived in Sheffield all my life but to be honest, Henderson's came to me late on. I had a moment of realisation when somebody asked if I wanted it with my pie – it was in The Cocked Hat down Attercliffe – and after saying 'what's that?', I soon realised that it would go with loads of things. You can even splash it in Bolognese, not that my parents (who are from Italy) would have done that! They moved to Sheffield in the 60s so I was born and bred here.

TONI MINICHIELLO, ATHLETICS COACH

ROAST CHICKEN DINNER

PREPARATION TIME: 5 MINUTES | COOKING TIME: 55 MINUTES, PLUS 10 MINUTES RESTING | SERVES: 4

FOR THE ROAST CHICKEN

1 lemon
Small bunch of fresh thyme
1.5kg chicken
2–3 cloves of garlic, crushed
1 tbsp olive oil
Sea salt and black pepper, to taste

FOR THE GLAZED CARROTS

1 large carrot or 6 baby carrots
50g butter
30g caster sugar
Pinch of salt

TO SERVE

Roast potatoes
Seasonal vegetables

FOR THE ROAST CHICKEN

Preheat the oven to 200°c.

Slice the lemon halfway through lengthways. Insert a sprig of thyme into the slit and place the lemon inside the cavity of the chicken.

Strip the leaves from the remaining thyme stalks, place them in a bowl and add the garlic. Pour in the olive oil, and blend everything together.

Place the chicken in a roasting tray and pour over the flavoured oil. Season the chicken generously with sea salt and black pepper.

Cover the chicken loosely with foil and roast for 20 minutes. Remove the foil and roast for another 20 minutes. Reduce the temperature to 180°c and roast for a further 15 minutes, or until the chicken is cooked through. It is fully cooked if the juices run clear when the bird is pierced in the thigh with a skewer.

Turn off the oven and let the chicken rest in the residual heat for at least 10 minutes. Remove from the oven, then carve.

FOR THE GLAZED CARROTS

Peel the large carrot or wash the baby carrots, then cut into attractive shapes. Place in a saucepan with enough water to just cover them and add the butter, sugar and salt.

Bring to the boil and cook until the carrots are tender and the liquid has reduced to a glaze. If there is still a lot of liquid left, remove the carrots and keep reducing, then return the carrots to the pan to heat through before serving. Check the seasoning and finish the carrots in the oven for extra colour if you like.

Serve the roast chicken with the glazed carrots and roast potatoes, as well as a good gravy made with Hendo's and any seasonal vegetables.

Photo: India Hobson

A roast dinner was the first thing my mum taught me to cook. That's the benchmark, I think, of whether you can cook or not. Maybe I shouldn't have impressed her and my wife by getting so good at it, though, because now that's my role every Sunday for the family. You have to have a splash of Hendo's in the gravy, 100%. My businesses across the city have always been about bringing people together, just like a roast really, and have matured with time as my tastes have changed. Seeing Sheffield progress and improve during that time has been brilliant.

JAMES O'HARA, ENTREPRENEUR AND PUBLICAN

TAGLIATELLE BOLOGNESE

PREPARATION TIME: 15 MINUTES | COOKING TIME: 1 HOUR 10 MINUTES | SERVES: 2

FOR THE BOLOGNESE

25g butter
50g onion, chopped
1 clove of garlic, chopped
400g lean minced beef
125ml beef stock
1 tbsp tomato purée
Glug of Henderson's Relish
Pinch of dried marjoram or oregano
100g mushrooms, diced
Salt and pepper

FOR THE PASTA

140g tagliatelle nests
OR
150g '00' flour, plus extra for dusting
1 egg and 2 yolks, lightly beaten

FOR THE BOLOGNESE

Place the butter in a pan over a medium heat, then when it has melted add the chopped onion and garlic. Cook for 4 to 5 minutes then add the beef and cook until lightly coloured, stir to break up the mince and brown it all evenly. Add the stock, tomato purée, Henderson's Relish and herbs.

Simmer the Bolognese for about 40 minutes until tender, then add the mushrooms and simmer for a further 5 minutes. Season to taste.

FOR THE PASTA

To make your own pasta, put the flour in a food processor with three quarters of the egg mixture and a pinch of salt. Blitz the mixture to large crumbs, which should come together to form a dough when squeezed. Add more egg if dry. Knead the dough on a lightly floured surface for 1 minute or until smooth. Cover with cling film and rest for 30 minutes.

Feed the first half of the dough through the widest setting on your pasta machine. Fold the pasta sheet into three, give the dough a quarter turn and feed it through the pasta machine again. Repeat this process once more then continue to pass the dough through the machine, progressively narrowing the rollers, until you have a smooth sheet of pasta.

Cut the pasta into long strips to make tagliatelle. Dust in a little flour and set aside until ready to cook. Alternatively, you can hang the tagliatelle until dry (an hour will be enough time) then store it in a sealed container in the fridge and use within a couple of days, or freeze for 1 month.

TO SERVE

Cook the tagliatelle in salted boiling water until done to your liking, bearing in mind that fresh homemade pasta will take much less time. Drain well then toss the cooked pasta with the Bolognese sauce and serve.

I'm Sheffield born and bred — my parents and grandparents were too — so I've seen lots of change in the city over time. I used to bake with my grandma, who lived near Park Hill, while mum and dad did their shopping in town, because it wasn't an exciting place for me back then! I think food is such an important part of where you choose to live and your community, so bringing more of that to the city in a fun and affordable way was the idea behind Peddler. There's so much diversity and choice in Sheffield now which is brilliant.

HEATHER GILBERTHORPE, PEDDLER MARKET

TOAD IN THE HOLE

PREPARATION TIME: 10 MINUTES | COOKING TIME: 50 MINUTES | SERVES: 4

FOR THE TOAD IN THE HOLE

4 good quality sausages

Splash of vegetable oil

2 medium eggs

65g plain flour

100ml milk

1 tsp fresh sage, chopped

Salt and pepper

FOR THE ONION GRAVY

25g butter

1 tbsp olive oil

1 bay leaf

2 sprigs of thyme

4 onions, sliced

1 tsp sugar

1 tbsp flour

200ml red wine

2 tsp red wine vinegar

500ml beef or vegetable stock

FOR THE TOAD IN THE HOLE

Preheat the oven to 200°c.

Put the sausages in a 20cm by 20cm roasting tin with a tablespoon of oil, toss them around and then cook for 15 minutes in the preheated oven until they are lightly browned.

Make the batter by whisking the eggs, flour and milk together until smooth, and then add the sage and seasoning.

Once the sausages are browned, take the tin out of the oven and carefully pour the batter over the sausages. It will sizzle so be careful! Place the tin back in the oven for 30 to 40 minutes until golden and crisp.

FOR THE ONION GRAVY

Melt the butter with the olive oil in a large frying pan over a medium heat, add the bay leaf and thyme then cook for 1 minute to infuse the flavours of the herbs. Add the onions and coat well in the butter and oil, sprinkle over the sugar and a big pinch of salt then slowly cook them down for 45 to 50 minutes, stirring occasionally until sticky and caramelised.

Add the flour and stir well, coating all of the onions. Cook for a minute then add the wine and vinegar. Turn up the heat and reduce the liquid by half, which should take about 2 minutes, whisking a little to ensure the flour doesn't form lumps at all. Pour in the stock, bring to the boil and cook for 6 to 8 minutes, until the gravy is thick enough to coat the back of spoon. If you cook it a bit too much and it gets too thick, add a splash of water. Season well and serve.

Serve the toad in the hole with the onion gravy and Henderson's Relish on the table for splashing over the top.

Photo: Leah Abdulla / Tim Cleasby Photography

Food has always been a massive part of my life in the fusion of our Indian and Sheffield family. We have Hendo's alongside the spices in our kitchen cupboards, which I think really complement each other, and also reflect who I am as a person. We also have to send Hendo's all over the place to family around the world! On the flip side, Sheffield has become a home to so many people from all over the world, and that exchange has created such a warm and friendly melting pot.

SAM CLEASBY, BLOGGER & RADIO PRESENTER

BEEF BURRITOS

PREPARATION TIME: 30 MINUTES | COOKING TIME: 45 MINUTES | SERVES: 8

8 flour or corn tortillas

500g cooked rice

FOR THE CHILLI

1 tbsp oil

1 large onion, diced

2 cloves of garlic, crushed

1 red pepper, diced

1 heaped tsp hot chilli powder (or 1 level tbsp mild chilli powder)

1 tsp paprika

1 tsp ground cumin

400g lean minced beef

200ml beef stock

300g tinned tomatoes

½ tsp dried marjoram

1 tsp sugar

Salt and pepper

30g tomato purée

300g tinned red kidney beans

FOR THE TOPPINGS

Your choice of avocado, tomatoes, soured cream, shredded lettuce, sliced red onion, grated cheddar, sliced red chilli and wedges of lime

FOR THE CHILLI CON CARNE

Put the pan over a medium heat, add the oil and leave it for 1 to 2 minutes until hot. Add the onion and cook, stirring fairly frequently, for about 5 minutes, or until the onion is soft. Add the garlic, red pepper, chilli powder, paprika and ground cumin. Give it a good stir, then leave it to cook for another 5 minutes, stirring occasionally.

Turn the heat up a bit, add the meat to the pan and break it up with your spoon or spatula. The mix should sizzle a bit when you add the mince. Keep stirring for at least 5 minutes, until all the mince is in uniform lumps and there are no more pink bits. Make sure you keep the pan hot enough for the meat to fry and become brown, rather than just stew. Add the beef stock to the mince along with the tinned tomatoes, dried marjoram, sugar and a good shake of salt and pepper. Add the tomato purée and stir the sauce well.

Bring the whole thing to the boil, give it a good stir then put a lid on the pan. Turn down the heat until it is gently bubbling and leave for 20 minutes. In the meantime, cook the rice. Check on the chilli occasionally to stir it and make sure the sauce doesn't catch on the bottom of the pan or dry out. If it does, add a couple of tablespoons of water and make sure that the heat is low enough. Add the kidney beans and cook for 5 more minutes.

FOR THE BURRITOS

Heat the tortillas by following the instructions on the packet. Pile some rice and chilli con carne in the centre of each tortilla and scatter over your choice of toppings. Fold over the ends and roll up to seal. Secure by wrapping one end with foil if you want. Dip into Henderson's Relish and eat immediately!

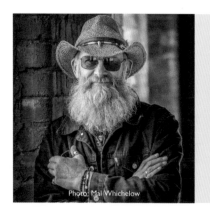

Photo: Mal Whichelow

Sheffield's very relaxed but at the same time there's a huge amount of talent here in the art and music scenes. I fell in love with the city when I came up to Psalter Lane Art College in '76 and everyone I met – from steelworkers to other students – was so accepting. Being under the radar in a way is a good thing; you're allowed to evolve outside the 'pressure cooker' environments of London or Manchester, say. At the Honeybee Blues Club I run, we do 10 to 15 gigs every month; there's plenty of quality to showcase.

MARTIN BEDFORD, POSTER ARTIST & PROMOTER

TOMATO SOUP

PREPARATION TIME: 15 MINUTES | COOKING TIME: 40 MINUTES | SERVES: 4

FOR THE VEGETABLE STOCK

3 sticks of celery

2 carrots

2 onions

1 leek

1 clove of garlic

1 bay leaf

1 sprig of thyme

2 peppercorns

FOR THE SOUP

1 onion

1 carrot

1 stick of celery

2 cloves of garlic

100g butter

2 tbsp tomato purée

100g flour

1 litre vegetable stock (see above)

4 tomatoes, chopped

1 bay leaf

1 sprig of thyme

FOR THE VEGETABLE STOCK

To make your own vegetable stock, grate all the vegetables and garlic into a large pan, cover with water and add the herbs and peppercorns. Bring to the boil, reduce the heat and simmer the stock for 10 minutes, then strain and reserve the liquid.

FOR THE SOUP

Make a mirepoix by finely dicing the vegetables and garlic, then sweat that in a pan with the butter until softened. Stir in the tomato purée and cook for 1 minute, then stir in the flour and cook to a sandy texture. Add the hot vegetable stock gradually, stirring everything well, until incorporated. Add the chopped tomatoes, bay leaf and thyme then simmer the soup for 30 minutes.

Strain the soup if you like, season to taste and then serve with a splash on Henderson's Relish on each bowlful.

Photo: Tess Bocking

I'm a journalist, writing about Sheffield's people and countryside for over 30 years, mainly in the Sheffield Telegraph. The Outdoor City's landscape and wildlife needs celebrating and supporting! As a foster carer I also shout out about all the Sheffield folk who help get local kids back on track. Our current toddler likes Hendo's with fish pie, and I help clear up all the mess afterwards. I once lived in Manchester, and when joining fellow Sheffielders for dinner, we'd make a point of all standing up before eating to salute the bottle of Hendo's waiting on the table.

DAVID BOCKING, JOURNALIST

Photo: Paul Cocker

ONE POT WONDERS

BRAISED BRISKET OF BEEF

PREPARATION TIME: 30 MINUTES | COOKING TIME: 2-3 HOURS | SERVES: 6

150ml vegetable oil
1kg brisket, trimmed
200g smoked bacon, chopped
250g carrots, diced
250g celery, diced
700g onions, diced
20 white peppercorns, crushed
4 bay leaves
4 sprigs of thyme
10 cloves of garlic, peeled
1 bottle of red wine
100ml Henderson's Relish
2 litres beef stock
200g tomato purée

FOR THE PUDDINGS
Sunflower oil
140g plain flour
4 eggs
200ml milk

Heat the oil in a deep heavy pan with a lid. Brown the brisket well then remove it from the pan and set aside. Add all the remaining ingredients except the wine, stock and tomato purée to the pan to brown, then return the brisket to the pan and add the wine, relish, stock and tomato purée. Cover the pan with the lid and braise until cooked. This will take 2 to 3 hours. Make the batter for the Yorkshire puddings.

After the cooking time, adjust the consistency of the sauce with a little more stock if necessary and correct the seasoning.

FOR THE PUDDINGS

Preheat the oven to 230°c (fan 210°c) and pour a little sunflower oil evenly into two four-hole Yorkshire pudding tins, or two twelve-hole non-stick muffin tins. Place the tins in the oven to heat through for 10 to 15 minutes.

To make the batter, put the plain flour into a bowl and beat in the eggs until smooth. Gradually add the milk and continue beating until the mixture is completely free from lumps. Season the batter with salt and pepper then pour it into a jug.

Remove the hot tins from the oven. Carefully and evenly pour the batter into the holes. Place the tins straight back in the oven and leave undisturbed for 20 to 25 minutes until the puddings have puffed up and browned evenly. Serve immediately.

TO SERVE

Place the meat in a suitable serving dish and then cover with the sauce.

As a chef, I find Henderson's Relish a great ingredient. It's especially good as a marinade for beef brisket, enhancing the flavours of the beef during cooking and providing a final dish that is both tender and full of flavour. Henderson's is local, it's available wholesale, and it's Sheffield. For Fischer's, our multi award-winning restaurant and The Prince of Wales, our posh sister pub, being near the city is good both in terms of sourcing ingredients and the university, where we work hard on student development. It's a nice spot to be in as a restaurateur.

MAX FISCHER, CHEF

CASSOULET AND CONFIT DUCK

PREPARATION TIME: 1 HOUR, PLUS 24 HOURS SOAKING | COOKING TIME: 3 HOURS | SERVES: 4

FOR THE CONFIT DUCK

6 cumin seeds
12 coriander seeds
3 juniper berries
50g flaky sea salt
4 duck leg and thigh joints
1 small bunch of thyme
1 sprig of rosemary
1 unpeeled clove of garlic, sliced
525g goose or duck fat
1 whole garlic bulb, halved
2 bay leaves
1 tsp black peppercorns

FOR THE CASSOULET

2 medium onions, diced
3 cloves of garlic, crushed
100g each carrot and celery, diced
200ml white wine
3 sprigs of thyme
750ml tomato passata
Glug of Henderson's Relish
500g haricot beans
Pinch of nutmeg
25g basil
15g parsley, chopped

FOR THE CONFIT DUCK

The day before cooking, put the cumin and coriander seeds in a dry pan and toast until they are slightly coloured and aromatic. Remove to a board and crush them with the blade of a knife. Crush the juniper berries and mix with the salt and seeds. Rub the mixture over the duck, scatter with the thyme, rosemary and sliced garlic then chill for 24 hours, turning two or three times as it marinates.

Soak the haricot beans in water and leave them for the same amount of time. Drain and rinse them before use.

The next day, preheat the oven to 150°c. Wipe the duck with kitchen paper and pat dry, but don't wash off the marinade. Put the duck in a deep pan and cover with the goose or duck fat, leaving about 25g for the cassoulet. Add the garlic bulb, bay leaves and peppercorns and cook for about 2 hours 30 minutes, or until the meat is falling away from the bone.

Remove the confit duck legs from the fat and heat an ovenproof frying pan. Add the duck legs, skin-side down, and cook for 4 minutes. Turn the legs over and transfer the pan to the oven for 30 minutes.

Meanwhile, make the pork belly according to the recipe on page 88.

FOR THE CASSOULET

Heat an ovenproof dish and fry the onions and garlic in the remaining duck fat until they are soft but not coloured, then add the carrot and celery and fry for a further 2 minutes. Add the white wine, thyme, tomato passata, Henderson's Relish and prepared haricot beans then put a lid on the dish. Place in the oven for approximately 1 hour, or until the beans are tender. Once the cassoulet is ready to come out of the oven, remove the sprigs of thyme and stir in the diced pork belly, nutmeg, basil and parsley.

Serve the crispy duck leg on top of the cassoulet.

Photo: Elly Lucas

We moved to Sheffield in 2010 to raise our kids. It was a city we already loved - for music, culture, and friendship. It's in a perfect location, as we travel a lot around Britain as professional folk musicians. Nancy lectures in music and James presents 'Thank Goodness It's Folk' on Sheffield Live Community Radio. Sheffield inspires us because it's a global city that feels like a village. It welcomes people from everywhere with open arms. Communities need to work together more than ever before. That's why we came, and that's why we stayed.

NANCY KERR & JAMES FAGAN, MUSICIANS

JAMAICAN CURRIED MUTTON

PREPARATION TIME: 2 HOURS 20 MINUTES │ COOKING TIME: 2 HOURS │ SERVES: 4

FOR THE SPICE BLEND

4 cardamom pods, split

1 tbsp each coriander and cumin seeds

½ tbsp each black peppercorns, fenugreek and mustard seeds

1 cinnamon stick, broken up

1 tbsp each ground ginger and turmeric

3 tsp ground allspice

FOR THE CURRY

1kg scrag end of mutton or lamb (or boneless shoulder if preferred)

1 lime, juiced

½ tsp salt

Sprig of thyme

1 small onion, thinly sliced

1 clove of garlic, finely chopped

½ scotch bonnet or 2 bird's eye chillies, finely chopped

Knob of butter

1 tbsp sunflower oil

1 medium potato

2 spring onions, sliced

Fresh coriander, roughly chopped

Cut the mutton or lamb into thick slices. Sprinkle the meat with the lime juice and salt, then leave to rest while you prepare the spice blend.

FOR THE SPICE BLEND

Lightly toast the whole spices in a dry frying pan, then grind them to a fine powder in a pestle and mortar or spice grinder. Stir in the ginger, turmeric and allspice.

FOR THE CURRY

Cover the meat with half of the spice mix. Strip the thyme leaves off the stalks and bruise with a knife, then mix them with the onion and garlic. Rub this into the meat, getting into all the cracks. Do the same with the chilli then set aside to marinate, preferably for at least 2 hours.

When you are ready to cook, heat a large saucepan over a medium to high heat then add a good knob of butter and the sunflower oil. Brown the meat in the pan while you peel and chop the potato, then stir it in. Pour in enough water to almost cover everything and bring to the boil, then reduce the heat and simmer for 2 hours, or until the meat is falling off the bone. Keep an eye on the sauce during this time, which should thicken and reduce, but if it gets too thick just add a little more water or stock. At the end of the cooking time, taste the curry, season with salt and then scatter in the spring onions. Cook for another few minutes, stir in the coriander and then serve.

The curry will improve over time, so you could leave it for a couple of days then reheat it to serve. Pork, chicken, goat, beef and fish all work well in this curry, but make sure you adjust the cooking times accordingly.

Food, Henderson's Relish and Sheffield are very important to me and interlinked in many ways. I grew up eating West Indian food, which wasn't available to most people. This confused me as a child. It's become part of the culture here now though, which is very satisfying and rewarding especially as I've played a part in developing food culture through my music. I feel as unique to Sheffield as Hendo's is. This city is the perfect foundation that allows me to express myself, my way. I'm confident for my children who will hopefully have even better experiences than I've had.

WINSTON HAZEL, DJ AND PRODUCER

JAMAICAN JERK CHICKEN, RICE AND BEANS

PREPARATION TIME: 10 MINUTES | COOKING TIME: 35 MINUTES | SERVES: 6

FOR THE JERK MARINADE

4 tsp smoked paprika

2 tsp allspice

1 tsp each chilli flakes, ground ginger and thyme

2 limes, juiced

2 tbsp olive oil

FOR THE JERK CHICKEN, RICE AND BEANS

8 chicken thighs or legs, bone in and skin on

1-2 tbsp olive oil

4 spring onions, finely sliced

3 cloves of garlic, grated

300g rice

400g tinned kidney beans

400ml tinned coconut milk

1 chicken stock cube

TO SERVE

Spring onions, sliced

Fresh chillies, sliced (optional)

1 lime, cut into wedges

FOR THE JERK MARINADE

Set half the lime juice aside, then mix all the ingredients for the marinade together in a large bowl, then add the chicken and coat thoroughly. Leave to marinate for 1 to 2 hours.

FOR THE JERK CHICKEN, RICE AND BEANS

Preheat the oven to 200°c. Heat up a large ovenproof frying pan and add a little olive oil. When the pan is hot, add the marinated chicken skin side down and fry for 2 minutes, then turn over and fry for 1 more minute on the other side. Transfer to a plate.

Turn the heat under the pan right down and add the spring onions and garlic. Fry for 2 minutes, then add the rice, kidney beans and coconut milk. Crumble in the chicken stock cube and add the lime juice that you set aside earlier.

Bring to the boil then add the chicken, skin side up. Cover with a lid or tin foil and place in the preheated oven for 15 minutes, then uncover and cook for a further 10 minutes.

TO SERVE

Scatter the chicken, rice and beans with sliced spring onion and chillies, if using, and serve with lime wedges as well as Henderson's for splashing on at the table.

Sheffield is the 'perfect place' for me. Since living here and discovering Henderson's Relish, I've used it in recipes taught to me by my Jamaican mum Valda. I'm a two-time Grammy nominated, World Music award-winning, four-time US Billboard Dance #1 artist and like Hendo's, I'm proud to be northern and black.

STEVE EDWARDS, SINGER/SONGWRITER

LAMB HOTPOT

PREPARATION TIME: 30 MINUTES | COOKING TIME: 2 HOURS 45 MINUTES | SERVES: 4

1kg scrag end or neck of lamb

4 lamb's kidneys, trimmed, cored and diced (optional)

50g dripping

4 large onions, very thinly sliced

1 bay leaf

Sprig of thyme

1 tbsp plain flour

1 tbsp Henderson's Relish

600ml lamb stock

1kg potatoes, peeled and thinly sliced

100g butter, melted

Salt and pepper

Brown the lamb in a heavy cast iron pot over a high heat in the dripping, then remove and do the same with the kidney. Set the meat aside and turn the heat down. Add the sliced onions, bay leaf and thyme and cook until the onion is softened and slightly caramelised. Stir in the flour and cook for 1 minute. Add the Henderson's and stock to the onions, bring to the boil and then reduce the heat to a simmer. Add the lamb and kidneys back to the pan and nestle in amongst the onions. Lay the sliced potatoes, overlapping, on top of the meat and onion layer, then brush the potatoes with melted butter and season with salt and pepper.

Cover the hotpot with a lid and cook in a moderate oven at approximately 180°c for 1 hour 30 minutes. After this time, remove the lid and brush the potatoes with butter again, turn the heat up and put the hotpot back in the oven without the lid to brown the potatoes for 30 minutes or so until golden and crisp.

Serve in the cooking pot at the table.

We were happy before our lottery win, and we were happy after. My wife Barbara and I won £7.6 million 19 years ago, and we gave £5.5 million of that away to friends, family and charities. I've also given a few bottles of Henderson's out so it gets all over the country!

My son-in-law's mum and dad live in Exmouth, and I met two ladies on a cruise who live in Southampton, so when I took them to the football they got some relish too. I like it with fish and chips, beans on toast, over hot pot and on my cooked breakfast.

RAY WRAGG, LOTTERY WINNER & PHILANTHROPIST

PORK SANCOCHO

PREPARATION TIME: 30 MINUTES | COOKING TIME: 2 HOURS | SERVES: 6

1kg pork shoulder
Vegetable oil
1 onion
1 red pepper
1 scotch bonnet
1 large sweet potato
1 green plantain
250g cassava or yucca
1 ½ litres chicken stock
Salt and pepper
15g parsley, chopped

First, dice the pork shoulder. If it still has the bone in, it may be easier to ask the butcher to prepare the meat for you. You can buy boneless pork shoulders though which make the job easier.

Prepare the vegetables by peeling and dicing the onion, deseeding and dicing the red pepper, finely dicing the scotch bonnet (leaving the seeds in if you like the heat!), peeling and dicing the sweet potato, dicing the plantain and peeling then dicing the cassava or yucca.

Sauté the diced pork in a large pan with a little oil for 5 to 6 minutes or until golden brown, then remove the meat with a slotted spoon and set aside on a plate. Fry the onion, red pepper and scotch bonnet for 3 to 4 minutes in the same pan. Add the pork back in along with all the other ingredients except the parsley.

Bring the mixture to a simmer and cook uncovered for 1 to 1 and a half hours, or until the pork is tender and the vegetables have softened and soaked up lots of flavour. Remove the pan from the heat, taste the sancocho, adjust the seasoning and then stir in the chopped parsley.

Serve with rice or just as it is, and of course, add a splash of Hendos!

I was born and bred in Sheffield then left it to study, but coming back with fresh eyes allowed me to discover pockets of culture and art all over the city. Those communities are really important to me, especially as Sheffield's Poet Laureate, because although my work has a global outlook there are inherent influences from the place I live in that come through. I think that's also true from a foodie perspective; some of my favourite food as a teenager was from a Caribbean restaurant on London Road, but I also like a splash of Hendo's on everything!

OTIS MENSAH, POET LAUREATE

SAUSAGE CASSEROLE

PREPARATION TIME: 30 MINUTES | COOKING TIME: 45 MINUTES | SERVES: 6

20ml sunflower oil

12 good quality pork sausages

2 onions, thinly sliced

2 cloves of garlic, crushed

400g tinned chopped tomatoes

300ml chicken stock

2 tbsp tomato purée

15ml Henderson's Relish

1 tsp dried mixed herbs

2 bay leaves

400g tinned butter beans

Salt and black pepper, freshly ground

Heat a tablespoon of the oil in a large non-stick frying pan and fry the sausages gently for 5 minutes, turning every now and then until nicely browned all over. Transfer them to a large saucepan or a flameproof casserole dish and set aside.

Place the onions in the frying pan and fry over a medium heat for 5 minutes until they start to soften, stirring often. There should be enough fat in the pan, but if not, add a little more oil. Add the garlic and cook for 2 to 3 more minutes, stirring frequently, until the onions turn pale golden brown. Stir in the tomatoes, chicken stock, tomato purée, Henderson's Relish, and herbs. Pour over enough water to cover everything, and bring it to a simmer.

Tip the mixture carefully into the dish with the sausages and return to a simmer, then reduce the heat, cover the pan loosely with a lid and leave to simmer very gently for 20 minutes, stirring from time to time.

Drain the beans and rinse them in a sieve under cold running water. Stir the beans into the casserole, and continue to cook for 10 minutes, stirring occasionally, until the sauce is thick. Season to taste with salt and freshly ground black pepper, then serve.

Our togetherness and unity as a city is something very special for me. Returning to Sheffield after the World Cup was amazing; my whole village came out for the party. Each time I come back nothing's changed, including my nan's stew and dumplings which is always made with Henderson's.

MILLIE BRIGHT, FOOTBALLER

STEW AND DUMPLINGS

PREPARATION TIME: 30 MINUTES | COOKING TIME: 2-3 HOURS | SERVES: 4

FOR THE BEEF STEW

30ml oil

25g butter

750g beef stewing steak, chopped into bite-size pieces

30g plain flour

175g baby onions, peeled

150g celery, cut into large chunks

150g carrots, cut into large chunks

2 leeks, roughly chopped

200g swede, cut into large chunks

500ml beef stock

Glug of Henderson's Relish

2 fresh bay leaves

15g fresh thyme leaves

15g fresh flat leaf parsley, chopped

Salt and black pepper, freshly ground

FOR THE DUMPLINGS

200g self-raising flour

Pinch of salt

100g suet

75ml cold water

Preheat the oven to 180°c.

FOR THE BEEF STEW

Heat the oil and butter in an ovenproof casserole dish and fry the beef until it is browned on all sides. Sprinkle over the flour and cook for a further 2 to 3 minutes. Then add all the vegetables and fry for 1 to 2 minutes. Stir in the stock, Henderson's Relish and herbs. Season with salt and freshly ground black pepper. Cover with a lid, transfer to the oven and cook for about 2 hours, or until the meat is tender.

FOR THE DUMPLINGS

Sift the flour and salt into a bowl. Add the suet and enough water to form a thick dough. With floured hands, roll spoonfuls of the dough into small balls. After it has been cooking for 2 hours, remove the lid from the casserole dish and place the dumplings on top of the stew.

Cover the stew, return it to the oven and cook for a further 20 minutes, or until the dumplings have swollen and are tender. If you prefer dumplings with a golden top, leave the lid off when returning the stew to the oven.

Photo: Medhurst

I've spent the last two decades working in the Sheffield music scene, alongside my career as a DJ during which I've performed with artists and at festivals all over Europe. I grew up in Sheffield though, so it's always been home and a bottle of Henderson's was always a staple on my mum's kitchen table, especially with stew and dumplings which was a favourite in our house. I'm thankful for the incredible support Sheffield has given us for The Tuesday Club, where I'm the resident DJ. What I like most about Sheffield people, though, is that they know how to have a proper party!

ANDY H, DJ

YEMENI CHICKEN

PREPARATION TIME: 1 HOUR 20 MINUTES | COOKING TIME: 20 MINUTES | SERVES: 4

8 chicken thighs
1 tsp coriander seeds
1 tsp cumin seeds
1 tsp black mustard seeds
1 tsp ras al hanout
Salt and cracked black pepper
3 tbsp sunflower oil
Henderson's Relish

FOR THE FLATBREADS

200g plain or wholemeal flour
¼ tsp salt
100ml warm water
2 tbsp oil (olive, sunflower or vegetable are all fine)

Rub the chicken thighs with the spices and oil, making sure they are well coated. Place in a suitable container and leave to marinate for 1 hour.

Preheat a grill to medium hot. Place the chicken into a roasting tray and colour under the grill until the skin has started to turn golden. Turn the thighs over and continue cooking until the meat is tender and can be pulled apart. Note that boneless chicken will cook quicker than bone-in chicken. You can use chicken breast for this recipe, but it can dry out if cooked for too long. If you want, shake some Henderson's Relish over the chicken while it's cooking to enrich the flavour even further.

FOR THE FLATBREADS

You can make these while the chicken marinates, then cook them while it grills. Place the flour and salt in a large bowl and trickle on the water bit by bit while bringing the dough together. Add the oil and knead the dough for about 5 minutes. You are aiming for a soft dough so if it's too sticky add a little more flour, and if it's too dry add a splash of water.

You can now cook the flatbreads straight away or leave the dough to rest for about half an hour.

Divide the dough into four balls and roll out on a lightly floured surface. Heat a large frying pan. Rub a little oil onto the surface, then cook each flatbread for about 2 minutes on the first side. It should puff up a little.

Flip the flatbread over using tongs and then cook for a couple of minutes on the other side. The flatbread should have turned lighter in colour and have a few brown char marks.

Keep the cooked flatbreads warm, wrapped in foil or a clean tea towel, until the others are cooked and the yemeni chicken is ready.

Serve the grilled chicken with the flatbreads and some pilaff rice if you like, garnished with flaked almonds and chopped tomatoes.

Sheffield is very dear to me, and although I've lived in other places I have always regarded it as my home town. It feels like a small village and is probably the only city where people talk to their neighbours!
It holds a unique position as a cohesive place, a city of sanctuary, somewhere that promotes diversity and cultural cohesion. I try to be a part of this and have many roles, from one of South Yorkshire's deputy lieutenants proudly serving Her Majesty, representing the British Muslim community, serving the local police commissioner's office and working within the wonderful interfaith community here.
IMAM SHEIKH MOHAMMAD ISMAIL DL, MUSLIM CHAPLAIN

PIES & PASTRIES

MEAT AND POTATO PIE

PREPARATION TIME: 20 MINUTES | COOKING TIME: 1 HOUR 30 MINUTES | SERVES: 4

FOR THE FILLING

50ml oil
400g stewing beef, diced
100g onion, finely chopped
10g plain flour
20g tomato purée
5ml Henderson's Relish
125ml brown beef stock
250g potatoes, peeled and diced
100g shortcrust pastry
Salt and pepper

FOR THE SHORTCRUST PASTRY

250g plain flour
125g margarine
Pinch of salt
40-50ml water
1 egg, beaten

FOR THE FILLING

Heat the oil in a pan and seal the diced beef. Add the chopped onion and gradually stir in the flour. Then add the tomato purée, relish and stock. Season the mixture with salt and pepper before adding the potatoes.

Simmer for 1 hour or until the beef is tender. Allow the filling to cool while you make the pastry, and then transfer into pie dishes.

FOR THE SHORTCRUST PASTRY

Season the flour with salt and then rub in the margarine so the mixture looks like breadcrumbs. Gradually add water until the pastry comes together into a smooth ball. Rest in the fridge for 20 minutes before using.

Roll out the chilled pastry to make lids for the pies, lay these over the filling and crimp the edges to seal them. Brush the lids with beaten egg then bake in the oven at 180°c for 30 minutes or until the pastry is golden bown.

Pie and Pea Nights were one of the first things to capture my heart when I moved here in 1995. I loved being introduced to this Sheffield treat and have since been to many events where it has been on the menu. As chaplain at St Luke's Hospice since 2007, I have been equally struck by the warmth and welcome of Sheffield's people. Their willingness to let me into their lives is a real privilege, and I see the strong connection many people have formed with me as a very precious gift from this wonderful place.

MIKE REEDER, CHAPLAIN

HAND-RAISED PORK PIE

PREPARATION TIME: 1 HOUR | COOKING TIME: 1 HOUR | SERVES: 4-6

FOR THE PIE FILLING

300g coarsely minced pork

200g rindless belly pork

¼ tsp chopped fresh thyme

½ tsp salt

½ tsp white pepper

½ tsp black pepper

½ tsp ground allspice

10 grates of nutmeg

1 small pinch of ground mace

1 tsp chopped fresh sage (optional)

FOR THE HOT WATER PASTRY

120ml water

100g lard, diced, plus extra for greasing moulds

200g plain flour

80g strong white flour

Pinch of salt

1 egg yolk, beaten

200ml white pork or chicken stock

1 leaf of gelatine

Preheat the oven to 180°c and grease a 15cm springform pie tin. Place all the ingredients for the filling into a large bowl and mix together really well.

FOR THE HOT WATER PASTRY

Place the water and lard into a saucepan over a medium heat. Place the flours and salt into a bowl. Make a well in the centre, and when the lard has melted and the water has almost boiled, pour the liquid into the flour. Beat well with a wooden spoon. When the pastry is cool enough to handle, turn out of the bowl and gently knead. Allow the pastry to cool further, then wrap in cling film and chill.

When cold, divide the pastry into quarters. Set one aside for the lid, then roll the rest out together into a large enough circle to fit the tin with some overhanging. Gently push the pork pie filling into the pastry case.

Roll out the pastry for the lid, brush the edge of the pie with egg yolk and place the lid over the filling, crimping the edges to seal the pastry. Brush the top with egg yolk and place the tin onto a tray. Make a small hole in the centre of the lid for steam to escape.

Bake the pie in the preheated oven for up to 1 hour. Check the pie after 40 minutes and if the pastry is getting too dark, cover the top with greaseproof paper. Remove the pie from the oven when a skewer or small knife inserted into the centre comes out hot and the juices run clear. Leave the pie for 10 to 15 minutes so it can rest and the pastry can set.

Meanwhile, bring the stock up to the boil and soak the gelatine for 5 minutes in cold water. Squeeze the gelatine out then stir it into the hot stock off the heat. Pass the stock through a sieve to remove any lumps. Gently pour the hot liquid into the pork pie through the hole in the top. Once the liquid reaches the top and bubbles up, gently tap the pie on a level surface to make sure the liquid is evenly distributed. Keep filling up to the very top if you like, then leave the pie to cool completely and enjoy!

When others might turn to chocolate, my go-to comfort food is a Waterall's pork pie, eaten with red cabbage and Hendo's. When I first came to Sheffield and tried one, I couldn't believe how good they were, and Waterall Pork Butchers in the Moor Market is still a very special place for me in the city.

PROFESSOR VANESSA, UNIVERSITY OF SHEFFIELD

CHICKEN AND MUSHROOM PIE

PREPARATION TIME: 30 MINUTES | COOKING TIME: 20-25 MINUTES | SERVES: 4

1 tbsp olive oil

450g chicken thigh, diced

75g button mushrooms, quartered

½ onion, chopped

½ clove of garlic, chopped

25g butter

1 tbsp plain flour

150ml warm milk

100ml chicken stock

Freshly grated nutmeg

Salt and pepper

1 tbsp fresh parsley, chopped

200g shortcrust pastry

½ egg, beaten

Heat the oil in a large pan and fry the chicken until it begins to turn white. Add the mushrooms and continue cooking until the chicken turns golden brown.

Remove from the pan and add the onion. Fry this for 3 minutes and then add the garlic and cook until it has softened. Add the onion and garlic to the chicken and mushrooms.

In the same pan, melt the butter then add the flour and cook to a paste. Gradually add the warm milk and stock with a pinch of nutmeg, whisking all the time until the sauce has thickened. Stir in the parsley, check the seasoning and then pour the sauce over the chicken. Leave the pie filling to cool a little in the dish you want to cook it in.

Roll out the pastry, moisten the edges of the pie dish and cover the filling, pressing down on the edges to seal it well. Crimp the pastry then brush it with the beaten egg to form a glaze. Make a slit or two in the centre to let out steam then bake the pie at 180°c for 20 to 25 minutes, or until the pastry is golden brown. Serve with mashed potato or chips, mushy peas and a bottle of Henderson's on the table.

Photo: Tim Taylor

I started working in the kitchen at The Notty over 12 years ago, first preparing the chips and mushy peas, and as we got busier I learned the recipes for all the pie fillings too. Although I didn't have any professional cooking experience at the beginning, the massive pies my aunty used to make for the whole family – always steak and potato – meant I knew what a proper home-cooked pie should be. The pies at The Notty are so popular because the fillings are all made from scratch, and served of course with a bottle of Henderson's on every table.

SUE BERESFORD, NOTTINGHAM HOUSE

COUNTRY TERRINE

PREPARATION TIME: 1 HOUR | COOKING TIME: 1 HOUR 15 MINUTES | SERVES: 6

75g butter
½ large onion, finely chopped
3 cloves of garlic, finely chopped
20ml medium sherry
1 tsp dried thyme
Pinch of grated nutmeg
1 tsp each of salt and pepper
500g pork, coarsely minced
200g chicken, minced
100g pork fat, minced
50g pistachios, shelled and chopped
1 tbsp chopped parsley
250g unsmoked pancetta or streaky bacon, rind removed

Heat the butter in a large pan then sweat the onion and garlic until tender. Add the sherry, thyme, nutmeg, salt and pepper. Bring to the boil and cook for 3 minutes, then remove from the heat and leave to cool.

Meanwhile, combine the pork, chicken, pork fat, pistachios and parsley, then mix well.

Lightly oil a loaf tin and then line with the bacon, letting the ends overhang the edges of the tin. Pack the meat in and cover with the remaining bacon, then wrap the tin in baking paper and cover tightly with foil.

Place the loaf tin in a roasting tray on the middle shelf of the oven, fill the tray half way up the loaf tin with hot water then slide the shelf back into the oven. Bake at 160°c for 1 hour and 15 minutes, or until the pork is cooked all the way through. If using a probe, the temperature should read 75°c. Leave the terrine to cool and then chill.

When cold, loosen the edges of the terrine with a palette knife dipped in hot water and turn the terrine out. Place on a board and cut into thick slices. Serve with crusty bread, cornichons, pickles and Dijon mustard.

Notes: confit duck can be added to the mixture as well as a little duck fat for extra flavour. Braised ham hocks can be added for a different texture. Baby leeks can be blanched, cooled and then laid down the length of the terrine in the centre to make the presentation a little more attractive. During the winter different game can be used instead of chicken. Minced duck, pigeon and pheasant all work very well in this recipe. Serve with crackers and Henderson's Relish for an elegant starter or lunch.

Photo: Robin Wood

Cooking is important to my family. My grandfather was a chef in the RAF. He was always travelling so as you can imagine his passion for international cuisine has been passed on down. We rarely had a roast growing up. Our Saturday tradition is Bolognese, saturated with Hendo's, not forgetting Yorkshire pudding starters the next day with the left over sauce. I mean, what's not to like? I put it on anything: whatever it is, a few drops definitely go in. You just need that staple orange label in the cupboard. My father-in-law who lives down south always receives a big one litre bottle.
MICHAEL MAY, KNIFE MAKER

PIEROGI

PREPARATION TIME: 45 MINUTES | COOKING TIME: 10-15 MINUTES | MAKES: 12

FOR THE DOUGH

3 eggs
200ml soured cream
400g plain flour
1 tbsp baking powder
¼ tsp salt

FOR THE SAUERKRAUT FILLING

50g butter
100g onion, chopped
300g sauerkraut, drained and minced
Salt and pepper
Splash of Henderson's Relish

FOR THE DOUGH

Beat the eggs and soured cream together until smooth. Sift the flour, baking powder and salt into the bowl and stir into the egg mixture until the dough comes together. Knead the dough on a lightly floured surface until firm and smooth. Divide the dough in half, then roll out one half to 0.25cm thickness. Cut into 7cm rounds using a scone cutter.

FOR THE SAUERKRAUT FILLING

Melt the butter in a frying pan over a medium heat. Stir in the onion and cook until translucent: about 5 minutes. Add the drained sauerkraut and cook for an additional 5 minutes. Season to taste with salt, pepper and a splash of Henderson's Relish, then transfer the filling to a plate to cool.

MAKING THE PIEROGI

Place a small spoonful of the sauerkraut filling into the centre of each round of dough. Moisten the edges with water, fold over to form a semicircle, and press down on the edges with a fork to seal.

Repeat this with the remaining dough, then bring a large pot of lightly salted water to the boil. Add the pierogi and cook for 3 to 5 minutes or until they float to the top. Remove with a slotted spoon.

Serve with soured cream, chopped dill and Henderson's Relish for dipping.

City of Sanctuary is a movement we founded here in Sheffield to make sure people seeking sanctuary are made to feel welcome and safe. Food is an important ingredient in our work at the Sanctuary. Our connectedness shows up in surprising ways, such as when heat from Sheffield's steel mills warmed the River Don to tropical temperatures, helping to germinate the seeds of fruit imported and eaten by Sheffielders, and creating the hundreds of fig trees that line the River Don! This fruit from other countries thrives here. So why not people from other countries also, living productive lives in Sheffield's welcoming, friendly environment?

INDERJIT BHOGAL, PRESIDENT OF CITY OF SANCTUARY

POTATO PANCAKES (LATKE)

PREPARATION TIME: 15 MINUTES | COOKING TIME: 10-20 MINUTES | SERVES: 4

1kg white potatoes
1 onion, finely chopped
3 eggs
100g plain flour
Salt and pepper
Oil, for frying

TO SERVE
Fresh dill, chopped
Soured cream
Caraway seeds

Line a large bowl with a clean, dry tea towel. Grate the potato into the bowl. Gather the edges of the towel together and squeeze as much of water out of the potatoes as you can. This will help to keep the mixture dry and the pancakes crispier.

Place the dry potato into a clean and dry mixing bowl along with the chopped onion. Beat the eggs together then add to the potato and onion. Stir in enough flour to form a thick, loose batter. Season the batter well with salt and pepper.

Heat enough oil to cover a large frying pan to a depth of 1cm. Place a spoonful of the batter into the hot oil. Control the heat so the pancake fries gently. Cook the pancake until golden and crisp and then gently turn over. Cook the second side of the pancake until golden, then remove and drain the pancake on paper towels. Repeat the process with the rest of the mixture, keeping the pancakes warm in the oven as you go.

Serve the pancakes as part of a meal – they go very well with crispy bacon, pork or smoked fish – or simply with chopped herbs, soured cream, a sprinkle of caraway seeds and a splash of Henderson's Relish as a snack.

Photo: Laurence Cendrowicz

I'm a mountaineer, author, and corporate inspirational speaker. I've climbed all over the world but I still love the trees and hills of Sheffield. I retired from mountaineering after making a solo ascent of a new route on the south face of Mera in Nepal, and have also written a book called Touching The Void which has been translated into 27 languages, made into a BAFTA winning film and adapted into a West End theatre production. When I get some time to relax, the Blades and The Byron pub in Sheffield are my favourites, especially given that the landlord is a Wednesday fan!

JOE SIMPSON, MOUNTAINEER

MUSHROOM AND ALE PIE

PREPARATION TIME: 30 MINUTES | COOKING TIME: 1-2 HOURS | SERVES: 6

60ml sunflower oil

300g shallots, peeled and halved if large (try and keep the root intact, so they keep their shape)

1 medium onion, thinly sliced

2 cloves of garlic, crushed

400g mixed mushrooms (such as chestnut, button, shiitake, Portobello)

330ml pale ale

Glug of Henderson's Relish

1 vegetable stock cube

30g tomato purée

30g redcurrant jelly

15g soft light brown sugar

1 tbsp fresh thyme leaves or 1 tsp dried thyme

2 bay leaves

3 tbsp cornflour

3 tbsp cold water

180g cooked and peeled chestnuts (vacuum packed is fine)

Flaked sea salt and ground black pepper

200g shortcrust pastry

Heat two tablespoons of oil in a large non-stick frying pan. Fry the shallots and onion over a medium heat for 10 to 12 minutes, or until softened and lightly browned, stirring occasionally. Add the garlic and cook for a few more seconds. Tip the mixture into a bowl and set aside.

Heat the remaining oil in the same frying pan and fry the mushrooms for 5 minutes, or until lightly browned. Stir in the ale, Henderson's Relish, crumbled stock cube, tomato purée, redcurrant jelly, brown sugar, thyme and bay leaves. Add the shallots and onions back to the pan. Season the mixture with a good pinch of salt and lots of ground black pepper.

Bring the liquid to a gentle simmer and cook for 15 to 20 minutes, stirring occasionally. Mix the cornflour with the water in a small bowl until smooth, then stir into the mushroom mixture. Cook for 1 to 2 minutes, or until the sauce thickens, while stirring.

Stir in the chestnuts and season to taste. Spoon the filling into a 1.5 litre pie dish and leave to cool before topping with the rolled out pastry.

Preheat the oven to 200°c and then bake the pie for 45 to 50 minutes, or until the pastry is pale golden brown and the filling is hot.

Sheffield has an underlying deep connection to me and my roots. It's where my studio is, where I've studied and where I've made a career. A past project of ours was redesigning Hendo's labels with the Tramlines line-up: to name just a few, we came up with "Pub-lunch Enemy" and "Annie Mac-and-Cheese". Hendo's doesn't feel mass produced. It gives ownership back to the people. It's a comfort food, intrinsic to the 'kick' in our local dishes and resonates with a Sheffield nostalgic civic pride that stems all the way back to the industrial era.

PAUL REARDON, PETER & PAUL DESIGN

BEEF EMPANADAS

PREPARATION TIME: 30 MINUTES | COOKING TIME: APPROX. 35 MINUTES | MAKES: 40

FOR THE SALSA

1 red onion, finely diced
1 serrano chilli, finely diced
Pinch of salt
Squeeze of lemon juice

FOR THE DOUGH

575g plain flour
1 tsp salt
75g chilled lard
200-250ml lukewarm water

FOR THE FILLING

2 tbsp olive oil
150g onion, diced
150g red or green pepper, diced
2 cloves of garlic, minced
1kg minced beef
125g green olives, sliced
125ml tinned tomatoes, blended
125g raisins
75ml dry sherry
1 tbsp Henderson's Relish
½ tsp Tabasco sauce
½ tsp ground cumin
¼ tsp dried oregano

FOR THE SALSA

Half an hour before you want to serve the empanadas, combine all the ingredients to make the salsa and set aside.

FOR THE DOUGH

Mix the flour and salt together in a bowl. Add the chilled lard and rub into the flour mixture using your fingers, a food processor or two round-bladed knives. Gently stir in the water a little at a time until the mixture forms a ball and isn't sticky anymore. Wrap the dough in cling film and chill in the fridge for at least 30 minutes.

FOR THE FILLING

Heat the olive oil in a large saucepan then add the onion, pepper and garlic. Sauté for 5 minutes, then add the minced beef to the pan, stir well and continue cooking for 5 minutes until beef is browned and fully cooked. Add the remaining ingredients and stir well so eveything is combined, cover the pan and lower the heat. Simmer for about 20 minutes. Set aside and let the mixture cool before filling the empanadas.

Heat the deep fat fryer to 185°c. Take the dough out of the fridge and divide into ten equal balls. On a lightly floured surface, roll out each dough ball into a thin circle. Place a few tablespoons of the empanada filling in the centre of each circle and fold half of the dough over to form a semicircle, sealing the edges by pressing down with a fork or twisting the edges over to form a seal.

Gently place one or two empanadas at a time in the hot oil (do not crowd the fryer) and cook until brown on each side: about 3 minutes per side. Remove from the oil and drain on a wire rack.

Serve warm with lots of salsa on the side.

I've never seen a pub without a bottle of Henderson's Relish, and on the rare occasions people ask for a Bloody Mary at mine I always make sure it gets Hendo's instead of that other stuff. I'd bath in it if I could. The best bit of my roast dinner is a gravy sandwich, because it's my job to make the gravy and I always do extra with loads of Hendo's lobbed in. My four year old is addicted to them now as well, so we sit and eat them watching a film on a Sunday afternoon.

DUNCAN SHAW, THE FAT CAT

SAUSAGE ROLLS

FOR THE FILLING

1 onion, finely diced
25g butter
6 sage leaves, finely chopped
½ tsp thyme, finely chopped
1 tsp parsley, finely chopped
500g sausage meat
Salt and pepper
500g puff pastry

FOR THE EGG WASH

2 egg yolks
1 tsp cold water
Pinch of salt

FOR THE FILLING

Sweat the onion in the butter without colouring until soft. Add the chopped herbs and allow the mixture to cool. Add the sausage meat, salt and pepper then mix well and transfer to a piping bag. Beat the eggs with the water and salt to make the egg wash.

TO ASSEMBLE

Roll out the puff pastry, pipe the sausage meat along the length of the pastry just off centre, then brush egg wash down the long side of the pastry next to the filling. Fold the pastry over the sausage meat and press down on the join with a fork to seal the edge.

Cut the sausage roll into the required lengths, egg wash the pastry and allow it to rest for 10 minutes in the fridge. Remove from fridge and egg wash again, then bake the sausage rolls at 180°c for 20 minutes until the pastry is golden brown and meat is cooked through.

Having grown up in the south, I fell in love with Sheffield's friendliness while here on a medical rotation in 2002…and never left! I am a GP, and both my children were born here. I spend much of my time encouraging and supporting new parents to use baby carriers up and down Sheffield's many hills and to be able to explore the Peaks. One of our favourite places is Stanage Edge; on New Year's Day we took warm sausage rolls in a Thermos and a bottle of Hendo's on a walk to the Stanage Pole. It was a bit hard to use in the wind!

DR ROSIE KNOWLES, GP

STEAK AND HENDERSON'S PASTY

PREPARATION TIME: 30 MINUTES | COOKING TIME: 30 MINUTES-1 HOUR | SERVES: 4

FOR THE SHORTCRUST PASTRY

250g plain flour

125g margarine

Pinch of salt

40-50ml water

1 egg, beaten

FOR THE FILLING

100g raw beef, chuck or skirt, cut into small pieces

100g potato, peeled and diced small

50g onion, chopped

50g swede, finely diced

15ml Henderson's Relish

Salt and pepper

FOR THE SHORTCRUST PASTRY

Season the flour with salt and then rub in the margarine so the mixture looks like breadcrumbs. Gradually add water until the pastry comes together into a smooth ball. Rest in the fridge for 20 minutes before using.

FOR THE FILLING

Cut the beef into small pieces. Peel then dice the potato, onion and swede, trying to keep everything evenly sized.

Mix all the filling ingredients together until they are well combined and season with Henderson's Relish, salt and pepper to taste.

TO ASSEMBLE

Roll out the shortcrust pastry 3mm thick and then cut it into rounds that are 12cm in diameter. Place a spoonful of filling on each round, then fold them in half and seal them by pressing the edges together. Crimp the edges of the pasties and brush the pastry evenly with the beaten egg.

Cook the pasties in a preheated oven at 160°c for 30 minutes to 1 hour then serve with more Hendo's on the side.

I was born in Sheffield and have been in Beehive Works as a grinder since '79. My job is to grind, shape and finish a piece of metal for whoever needs it doing; I work for different firms all over the city. Considering it's such an industrial place, one of the best things about Sheffield is you can walk it, cycle it, catch a bus and get straight out into countryside. I've got a boat – a proper motor cruiser – that I stop in over the weekend. It's a good place to be for the outdoors.

BRIAN ALCOCK, METAL GRINDER

STEAK, STILTON & GUINNESS PIE

PREPARATION TIME: 1 HOUR 20 MINUTES | COOKING TIME: 2 HOURS 30 MINUTES, PLUS CHILLING OVERNIGHT | SERVES: 4

FOR THE PASTRY

190g butter, diced
190g lard, diced
760g plain flour
Pinch of salt
190g egg, beaten

FOR THE FILLING

500g stewing steak, diced
100g flour
Salt and pepper
100g butter
1 onion, chopped
1 clove of garlic, chopped
1 carrot, chopped
2 sticks of celery, chopped
100g button mushrooms
Sprig of thyme
250ml Guinness or ale
2 tbsp Henderson's Relish
½ tin of chopped tomatoes
1 litre beef stock
150g stilton
1 egg yolk, beaten

FOR THE PASTRY

Place the fat, flour and salt into a suitable bowl or a food processor then either rub in by hand or pulse in the mixer until the mixture resembles fine breadcrumbs. Stir in the egg using a table knife to form a soft dough. It shouldn't be sticky, but if it is a little dry add a drop or two of water.

Lightly knead the pastry and then cut off a third. Flatten both pieces out and wrap well in cling film. Chill in the fridge overnight.

FOR THE FILLING

Coat the meat in seasoned flour and heat the butter in a pan. Brown the meat in batches in the butter. Add the vegetables and thyme to the pan and brown lightly. Stir in the Guinness, Henderson's, tomatoes and stock, bring to the boil, cover and simmer for 1 hour 30 minutes on the hob or in the oven. When the meat is tender, chill the filling, preferably overnight.

TO ASSEMBLE

Roll the larger piece of pastry out to roughly the thickness of a pound coin. Lightly grease a suitable pie dish and dust with flour. Lay the pastry into the dish with some overhanging the edges. Fill the pie dish with the cold filling. Crumble the stilton over the top, pushing it in slightly.

Roll out the smaller piece of pastry to make a lid. Brush the edges with egg, lay it over the filling and gently push the edges together, then trim them neatly with a small sharp knife. Crimp using a fork or by hand.

Brush the top of the pie with the egg then place it in the fridge for 10 minutes. Egg wash again to give the pie a nice glossy finish, and use a small cutter or sharp knife to make a small steam hole in the middle of the lid.

Place the pie onto a baking sheet and bake at 200°c until the pastry is golden and crisp, and the filling is piping hot. Serve the pie with your favourite accompaniments and sides.

I started working at the University of Sheffield in 1992 and, being from Oldham, I had never heard of Henderson's Relish! I was quickly introduced and it soon became a personal favourite, especially with pies. Many international students I know have also become loyal Hendo's fans, creating a global following for this iconic condiment.

DAVID MCKOWN MBE, UNIVERSITY OF SHEFFIELD

VEGETABLE SAMOSAS

PREPARATION TIME: 10 MINUTES, PLUS 30 MINUTES RESTING | COOKING TIME: 45 MINUTES | SERVES: 6

FOR THE FILLING

1 tbsp vegetable oil

1 onion, finely chopped

2 cloves of garlic, crushed

2 tsp curry powder, or your own spices according to taste

1 potato (about 150g), finely diced

1 carrot (about 100g), finely diced

100g frozen peas

100ml vegetable stock

FOR THE PASTRY

225g plain flour

2 tsp sea salt

30g vegetable oil

100ml water

2 litres vegetable oil

FOR THE FILLING

Heat the oil in a frying pan, add the onion and garlic, mix in the spices and fry for 10 minutes until the onion is soft. Add the vegetables and stir well until coated with the spices. Add the stock, cover and simmer for 30 minutes until cooked. Leave to cool.

FOR THE PASTRY

Mix the flour and salt in a bowl. Make a well in the centre, pour in the oil and water and combine to make a firm dough. Knead the dough on a floured surface for 5 to 10 minutes until smooth, then roll into a ball. Wrap the dough in cling film and rest at room temperature for 30 minutes.

Divide the pastry into 15 equal portions. Roll out thinly to equal lengths. Place a heaped teaspoon of filling on the top left side of the pastry and fold over into a triangle as shown in the photo.

Heat the oil to 180°c in a large deep saucepan. The oil should come one third of the way up the pan. Deep fry the samosas in batches for 3 to 4 minutes until crisp and brown. Remove and drain on kitchen paper before serving with Henderson's on the side for dipping if you like.

Photo: Emma Betts

I moved to Sheffield 30 years ago, back to my Gran's home town. I love that, as a city, we try out new ideas without forgetting what we've learnt from the past. I work for Sheffield Young Carers and our Young Carers Action Group met with the Prime Minister to demand rights for young carers across the country, and took a bottle of Henderson's Relish as a gift from our city. Our young people speak up and speak out – I am proud to work with the amazing young carers who exemplify the gut and vibrancy of Sheffield.

SARA GOWEN, SHEFFIELD YOUNG CARERS

THE WORTLEY GAME PIE

PREPARATION TIME: 2 HOURS, PLUS 12 HOURS MARINATING | COOKING TIME: 35-40 MINUTES | SERVES: 1-2

300g venison, diced

FOR THE MARINADE
4 juniper berries, crushed
2 bay leaves
2 cloves of garlic, crushed
4 sprigs of thyme
150ml red wine
6 black peppercorns

FOR THE FILLING
2 shallots, peeled and halved
110g carrot, diced
50g plain flour
25g tomato purée
500ml beef stock

FOR THE HOT WATER PASTRY
75g lard
100ml hot water
300g plain flour
1 tsp salt
1 egg, beaten

FOR THE MARINADE
Combine all the ingredients for the marinade, transfer them into a sealable bag or container and place the venison in the marinade. Leave it to marinate overnight in the fridge.

FOR THE FILLING
Take the venison out of the marinade (make sure to keep this) and pat dry on a clean cloth. Fry the venison in hot oil until browned and season with salt and pepper. Add the shallots and carrots and fry for a further 2 minutes. Add the flour and fry until slightly browned, then add the tomato purée and mix everything together.

Strain the marinade and add it to the pan, stirring so that no lumps form. Add the hot stock a little at a time to create a sauce (you might not need all the stock).

Simmer for about 1 hour or until the venison is tender. Taste, adjust the seasoning and then allow the mixture to cool.

FOR THE HOT WATER PASTRY
Melt the lard in the hot water, then mix the liquid with the flour and salt to form pastry.

TO ASSEMBLE
Grease and flour a pork pie tin then line it with the pastry by gently pressing and moulding. Fill with the venison mixture. Roll out a pastry lid and place it on top, seal the edges by crimping them then brush with the beaten egg. Bake in the oven for 35 to 40 minutes at 180°c or until the pastry is golden brown.

In running The Famous Sheffield Shop I've got to know so much about Sheffield's international reputation for quality. The shop has welcomed visitors from all over the world, including every state in the USA. Hendo's, of course, is in regular use at the Iseard household. Over the years we've amassed a collection of special edition bottles, jealously guarded by my older son. One was brought out to celebrate Jessica Ennis's gold, another for Sheffield United's return to the Premiership. Matt Cockayne's Hendophant is a personal favourite, raising funds for The Sheffield Children's Hospital.

PAUL ISEARD, BUSINESS OWNER

VEGAN DISHES

YORKSHIRE PUDDING WITH GRAVY

PREPARATION TIME: 10 MINUTES | COOKING TIME: 25 MINUTES | SERVES: 12

100g plain flour
100g gram flour
2½ tsp baking powder
¼ tsp table salt
¼ tsp black salt
1 tsp cider vinegar
360ml water
120ml aquafaba
Vegetable oil

FOR THE GRAVY

2 tbsp olive oil
1 onion, chopped
2 cloves of garlic, minced
1 carrot and 1 stick of celery
100g plain flour
150ml red wine
50ml Henderson's Relish
1 litre 'beef' or mushroom stock
Fresh rosemary and thyme

Combine the two flours, baking powder and table salt in a bowl. In a separate jug, whisk the black salt, cider vinegar, water and aquafaba together. Pour the liquid mixture into the dry ingredients and whisk together until smooth. Transfer the mixture back into a jug for easy pouring and rest in the fridge for 10 minutes.

Preheat the oven to 220°c. Using a muffin tray, add approximately one and a half tablespoons of oil into each well and swirl the tray to coat the sides. Heat the tray in the oven for 10 minutes after which the oil should be smoking hot.

Remove the batter from the fridge and pour some into the centre of each muffin well. Fill them up to at least two thirds full. Place the tray back into the oven for 25 minutes. The Yorkies should have risen and turned golden brown.

Remove from the oven and allow to cool slightly before serving. Meanwhile, heat the gravy and ladle generously over a pile of Yorkshire puddings. Alternatively, fill a gravy jug and serve it on the side.

FOR THE GRAVY

Finely chop all the vegetables while you heat the oil in a large saucepan. Sauté the onion, garlic, carrot and celery. Add the flour and cook out for 1 minute. Whisk in the red wine, Henderson's Relish and stock, ensuring there are no lumps. Bring the gravy up to the boil and then reduce to a simmer for 10 minutes. Add some chopped herbs with a pinch of salt and pepper to taste.

We eat Yorkies all the time as a family – my partner Laura is brilliant at making them, and my three sons love them – always with mash and Hendo's. Incidentally, Hendo's is a great way to get your kids eating more veg; mine love halved cherry tomatoes drizzled with it.

ALEX DEADMAN, TRAMLINES

NOT FISH AND CHIPS

PREPARATION TIME: 45 MINUTES, PLUS AT LEAST 1 HOUR FREEZING | COOKING TIME: 10 MINUTES | SERVES: 4

FOR THE F*SH

4 blocks firm tofu, drained and dried

510g tinned banana blossom, drained and dried

4 nori sheets

FOR THE BATTER

125g plain flour, plus extra for dredging

½ tsp salt and pepper

½ tsp turmeric

230ml sparkling water

FOR THE CHIPS

1 litre vegetable oil, suitable for frying

1kg Maris Pipers, washed and cut into chunky sticks

Salt and vinegar

FOR THE F*SH

Line a flat tray that will fit in your freezer with greaseproof paper. Using scissors, cut a fish fillet shape out of each nori sheet and place on the lined tray. Lay a full banana blossom in the centre of each nori sheet, and stuff with about 50g of firm tofu. Mould them to fit the nori sheets, keeping an even thickness from top to bottom. Cover the fish shapes with cling film and freeze for at least 1 hour. Prepare them in advance and freeze overnight, or keep them in your freezer for up to 3 weeks.

FOR THE BATTER

Place all the dry ingredients in a bowl, then slowly add the sparkling water while whisking until there are no lumps and a smooth batter has formed. Place in the fridge until needed.

FOR THE CHIPS

In a deep fryer or pan, bring the vegetable oil up to 100°c. Add the potato and fry for about 4 minutes, until softened to the touch but not coloured. Drain on kitchen towel, allowing the potato to steam dry and cool completely. Refrigerate or freeze until ready to use.

TO SERVE

Bring the oil up to 190°c while you prepare the 'fish' by coating each piece in seasoned flour, then submerging them in the batter. Gently shake off any excess then lay the pieces into the oil away from yourself.

Fry the 'fish' for about 10 minutes until golden brown and piping hot. Remove from the fryer and drain on kitchen towel. Gently lower the cooled potato into the oil, and cook until floating and golden in colour. Drain on kitchen towel then season with salt and vinegar. Cut a lemon into wedges, load up the plates with chips and top each pile with a 'fish' fillet. Douse with Hendo's and a squeeze of lemon juice.

Photo: Mark Howe

One of the great things about Sheffield is the large creative community of artists living and working in the centre of the city. Henderson's Relish was the first building that I drew in the city. At the time I lived in London and was initially drawn to the bright orange sign on the tumble-down diminutive factory, dwarfed by its modern neighbours. I love that a sauce can mean so much to people and I think it says a lot about Sheffield that a condiment can become an icon of the city.

JO PEEL, ARTIST

'BACON' SANDWICH AND SCRAMBLED 'EGGS'

PREPARATION TIME: 15 MINUTES, PLUS 1 HOUR IF MAKING SEITAN | COOKING TIME: 5 MINUTES | SERVES: 4

Loaf of bread
Vegan butter/spread
Henderson's Relish

FOR THE 'BACON'

1 portion of seitan (see page 150)
50g smoked paprika
50g nutritional yeast
50ml maple syrup
200ml vegetable oil

FOR THE 'EGGS'

400g firm tofu
½ tsp black salt
½ tsp turmeric
Pinch of salt
Pinch of pepper
Chives, chopped

FOR THE 'BACON'

Instead of cutting the seitan loaf into cubes, slice it into 16 thin strips using a sharp knife. Combine the smoked paprika, nutritional yeast, maple syrup and oil together with a whisk and marinate the slices of seitan in the mixture.

FOR THE 'EGGS'

Mix all of the ingredients together, crushing the tofu gently to different size pieces, ensuring a scrambled egg-like texture.

TO SERVE

Cut two thick slices of bread and butter them. Bring two frying pans up to a medium heat, add four slices of 'bacon' to one and a generous helping of the tofu 'egg' mixture into the other. Cook both gently until piping hot, flipping the 'bacon' once and stirring the eggs occasionally.

Remove the 'bacon' from the pan and place the slices onto one half of the buttered bread, splash with Henderson's Relish, and pop the other slice of bread on top.

Cut in half and serve next to a mountain of scrambled 'eggs'.

Working with BBC Radio Sheffield since 1984 has enabled me to stay here in the Steel City all my life. Hendo's is important to us all, of course, you can't go anywhere without seeing the famous orange label. I think we all have a vision of Henderson's as being a bit like Willy Wonka's chocolate factory but I remember visiting the old place to do a live interview for radio a few years back. My remit was to uncover their big secret ingredient but all I saw was a small room with a huge open vat of sauce in the middle… and of course they were sworn to secrecy about what that magic ingredient really was.

RONY ROBINSON, WRITER

CAULIFLOWER 'CHEESE'

PREPARATION TIME: 20 MINUTES | COOKING TIME: 45 MINUTES | SERVES: 8

FOR THE 'CHEESE' SAUCE

150g potato, peeled and cut into 1cm cubes

150g carrot, peeled and cut into 1cm slices

70g nutritional yeast

½ tsp smoked paprika

1 tsp garlic powder

1 tsp onion powder

2 tsp salt

3 tbsp lemon juice

150ml soy milk

FOR THE CAULIFLOWER

4 heads of cauliflower

2 tbsp olive oil

Salt

FOR THE 'CHEESE' SAUCE

Steam or boil the potatoes and carrots until very soft (steaming means they won't absorb as much water so the consistency may be easier to manage).
Once cooked, allow the vegetables to cool and steam off slightly, then transfer into a large bowl and add 100ml of water along with all of the other ingredients. Using a stick blender, blitz everything together until the mixture is smooth and velvety. Add more water to thin the sauce out if needed, and more nutritional yeast to taste.

FOR THE CAULIFLOWER

Remove the leafy exterior of the cauliflowers and discard. Cut the cauliflower into florets then lightly coat with olive oil and season with a pinch of salt. Preheat the oven to 180°c and bake the florets until they begin to soften, for about 10 minutes.

TO ASSEMBLE

Place the roasted cauliflower into a large, deep baking dish. Cover completely with the sauce and bake in the oven at 200°c for 20 minutes, until the surface is golden and bubbling. Remove from the oven and sprinkle with fresh herbs of your choice before serving with Henderson's Relish on the side.

I 'migrated' north 16 years ago, so Sheffield is very much my proudly adopted home. It's such a dynamic and culturally diverse city, but remains modest. Sheffield allows me to indulge my passion for being outdoors, particularly walking and my allotment. Growing and cooking vegetarian food is a big part of daily life; cauliflower cheese is actually our daughters' favourite meal and as a coeliac Henderson's is a great gluten-free accompaniment for me! I regularly smuggle 'Yorkshire relish' south to Devon for my 90 year old 'Strong and Northern' Sheffield uncle, who drinks it straight from the bottle.

DR NOREEN WEST, SHEFFIELD CHILDREN'S HOSPITAL

POTSTICKER DUMPLINGS

PREPARATION TIME: 50 MINUTES | COOKING TIME: 10 MINUTES | SERVES: 6

400g vegan dumpling wrappers

70g vital wheat gluten

Cornflour (for dusting)

300g tinned black beans

130g quinoa

1 tbsp sesame oil

2 tbsp soy sauce, or relish

2 cloves of garlic

20g ginger, chopped

30g each of spring onion and mushroom, chopped

1 carrot and 1 shallot, peeled and chopped

1 tbsp sugar

½ bunch of fresh coriander

1 tsp Szechuan powder

FOR THE DIPPING SAUCE

100ml each of sesame oil, soy sauce/relish and black vinegar

50g sugar

20ml chilli oil

2 star anise

1 tbsp each Szechuan peppers and sesame seeds

1 large dried orange rind

Place all the ingredients except the wrappers, vital wheat gluten and cornflour into a food processor. Blend for 5 minutes until the desired consistency is reached. Transfer the mixture to a large bowl and stir in the vital wheat gluten until dough forms. Cover with cling film and rest in the fridge for 10 minutes.

Using a teaspoon, place a small amount of the chilled filling into the centre of each wrapper. Using the tip of your finger, dampen one half of the edge of the wrapper with water, then fold the wrapper over the filling to encase the dumpling and create a semicircle shape. Gently but firmly seal the dumplings, pushing out any air from the centre as you work your way around. Place each dumpling on a lined tray and dust lightly with a little cornflour to prevent them sticking together. At this point the dumplings can be frozen until ready to cook.

FOR THE DIPPING SAUCE

Place all the ingredients except the sesame seeds into a saucepan and bring to the boil. Whisk occasionally to dissolve the sugar and prevent burning. Reduce the heat to a low simmer and leave the sauce to infuse for 10 minutes. Strain the mixture through a sieve and discard the solid ingredients. Add the sesame seeds and then cool before use.

TO SERVE

Bring a non-stick sauté pan with a lid up to a medium heat, add a little oil and place the dumplings into the pan. Gently cook for a few minutes until the base of the dumplings turns golden brown. Add about 100ml of water to the pan and cover with the lid.

Cook for a further 5 minutes or until the dumplings are soft and piping hot all the way through. Drain the dumplings and place them onto a plate or bowl, spoon over the sauce and garnish with chopped spring onions.

Photo: Chris Etchells

I make potstickers all the time, and have even used Henderson's Relish as a substitute for soy sauce and similar Asian ingredients. It's really good to have as a cupboard staple. Hendo's is just one of the many, many things I've embraced about my adopted home. I moved to Sheffield when I was 18 for college and was only supposed to stay a year, but never left. I love the city so much that it immediately felt like home, and I've been lucky enough to live here ever since, and to work for The Star over the last eight years.

ELLEN BEARDMORE, JOURNALIST & FOOD WRITER

POUTINE

PREPARATION TIME: 15 MINUTES, PLUS OVERNIGHT RESTING | COOKING TIME: 30 MINUTES | SERVES: 4

FOR THE 'CHEESE' CURDS

250g macadamia nuts, soaked overnight

30ml lemon juice

1 tbsp cider vinegar

3 cloves of garlic, minced

1 tbsp olive oil

90ml water

1 tsp salt

½ tsp black pepper

Fresh rosemary, chopped

Fresh thyme, chopped

1 tbsp nutritional yeast

FOR THE CHIPS

1 litre vegetable oil, suitable for frying

1kg Maris Pipers, washed and cut into chunky sticks

Salt and vinegar

TO SERVE

1 portion of gravy (see page 150)

Fresh chives, chopped

Henderson's Relish

FOR THE 'CHEESE' CURDS

Using a high-powered blender, combine all the ingredients until a smooth mixture has formed. Place a cheese cloth into a sieve, positioned over a sink or large bowl. Transfer the curds into the cheese cloth and gather the corners the centre, bunch together and twist to squeeze out excess liquid from the 'cheese' inside. Secure the ball with an elastic band and rest in the fridge overnight.

Grease a baking tray with olive oil and preheat the oven to 180°c. Remove the 'cheese' from the fridge and carefully unwrap it. Place on the tray and bake for 30 minutes. The cheese should turn golden brown. Remove from the oven and allow to cool completely before crumbling into curds.

FOR THE CHIPS

In a deep fryer or pan, bring the vegetable oil up to 100°c. Add the potato and fry for about 4 minutes, until softened to the touch but not coloured. Drain on kitchen towel, allowing the potato to steam dry and cool completely. Refrigerate or freeze until ready to use.

TO SERVE

Pile the chips into a bowl and crumble large pieces of the baked curds on top. Ladle a generous helping of hot gravy over everything, then finish with the chives and a few dashes of Henderson's Relish.

The main thing that kept me in Sheffield was the emerging food scene – a blank canvas that was being filled in rapidly. The city has the feel of a small village but is also a melting pot of cultures, and is such an open platform for trying different things. At the same time, there's a strong loyalty to things like Hendo's that I find myself sticking with too. I've used Hendo's since I first came to Sheffield because it's such an inclusive condiment that opened the door to vegan seasoning for me, and it just goes with everything.

ADAM CLARK, MAKE NO BONES

SEITAN AND RED WINE PIE

PREPARATION TIME: 2 HOURS | COOKING TIME: 1 HOUR 45 MINUTES | SERVES: 6

FOR THE SEITAN

500g vital wheat gluten

4 tbsp smoked paprika

2 tbsp each garlic and onion powder

1 tsp salt

1 tbsp black pepper

50ml each oil and tomato ketchup

2 tbsp each soy sauce and Henderson's Relish

1 tbsp vegan 'beef' stock

FOR THE RED WINE GRAVY

2 tbsp olive oil

1 onion, chopped

2 cloves of garlic, minced

1 carrot and 1 stick of celery

100g plain flour

150ml red wine

50ml Henderson's Relish

1 litre 'beef' or mushroom stock

Fresh rosemary and thyme

TO SERVE

1 pack of Jus-Rol puff pastry

Splash of soy milk

FOR THE SEITAN

Mix the dry ingredients together in a bowl and combine the wet ingredients in a jug. Create a well in the centre of the dry mixture and pour in the wet ingredients plus 1.5 litres of water. Bring together and knead for 5 minutes until the gluten has activated and a smooth and glossy dough has formed. Place the dough into a baking tray lined with greaseproof paper. Bake in the oven at 180°c for 1 hour, then leave to cool completely. Cut the seitan into 1cm cubes ready for use.

FOR THE RED WINE GRAVY

Finely chop all the vegetables while you heat the oil in a large saucepan. Sauté the onion, garlic, carrot and celery. Add the flour and cook out for 1 minute. Whisk in the red wine, Henderson's Relish and stock, ensuring there are no lumps. Bring the gravy up to the boil and then reduce to a simmer for 10 minutes. Add some chopped herbs with a pinch of salt and pepper to taste.

Stir the seitan cubes into the gravy and cool the pie filling completely in the fridge.

Set out six 11½ cm enamel pie pans and roll out the pastry. Cut out rectangles large enough to line the individual pans and six slightly smaller rectangles to use as lids. Press the pastry bases firmly into the corners of the pans and along the rims.

Remove the red wine gravy mix from the fridge and fill each pie to the brim, but make sure you leave enough space to seal the lids to the bases. Brush the edges of the pastry with a little water, lay the lid over the pie and use your thumb or a fork to gently crimp the pastry together.

Brush each pie with a little soy milk to glaze, then bake in the oven at 200°c for 30 minutes, or until golden brown and piping hot throughout.

I got involved with the Ramblers quite a few years ago, and was part of the campaign for access to Sheffield moorland which came to fruition in 2004; the movement had been going in Sheffield since the early 1900s. I think the outdoors is vital to us; one third of the city is in the Peak District National Park, and no matter where you live in Sheffield there's some greenery. Henderson's Relish is linked to going into the hills for me, because when you get back from a walk and have a really good home-cooked meal, Henderson's just makes it.

TERRY HOWARD, SHEFFIELD RAMBLERS & ACCESS CAMPAIGNER

'MEATBALLS' IN TOMATO SAUCE

PREPARATION TIME: 1 HOUR (PLUS RESTING) | COOKING TIME: 20 MINUTES | SERVES: 6

FOR THE 'MEATBALLS'

70g vital wheat gluten

300g tinned black beans, drained

130g quinoa, cooked and cooled

1 onion, chopped

2 tbsp each Henderson's Relish, olive oil and tomato paste

3 tsp dried oregano

1 tsp dried parsley

2 tsp beetroot powder

4 tbsp nutritional yeast

3 tbsp fresh basil

¼ tsp each salt and black pepper

FOR THE SAUCE

2 tbsp olive oil

1 onion, finely minced

2 cloves of garlic, finely minced

50ml red wine

1 tbsp tomato purée

2 tbsp Henderson's Relish

600g tinned chopped tomatoes

1 tsp oregano and thyme, chopped

4 tbsp nutritional yeast

1 bunch of basil, sliced

FOR THE 'MEATBALLS'

Place all the ingredients except the vital wheat gluten into a food processor and blend the mixture for a few minutes, until all the large pieces have broken down. Transfer the mixture into a large bowl and add the vital wheat gluten, kneading gently to incorporate it completely. When a meat-like dough has formed, shape the mixture into 25g balls.

Heat a frying pan with a little vegetable oil and add the meatballs in batches without overcrowding the pan. Sear the balls until golden brown and drain on paper towels. Set aside until ready to serve.

FOR THE SAUCE

Add the oil, onion and garlic to a large heavy-based pan. Sauté until translucent then add the red wine, tomato purée and Henderson's Relish. Simmer for a minute or two, then add the chopped tomatoes, oregano, thyme and nutritional yeast. Simmer for 20 minutes then remove from the heat. Using a stick blender, blitz the sauce to your desired consistency. Add salt and pepper to taste and finish with chopped fresh basil.

If you prefer a chunkier sauce, reserve one tin of the chopped tomatoes and add them back in after the rest of the sauce has been blended. Then bring the sauce back up to a simmer and cook for a further 5 minutes.

TO SERVE

Bring a large pot of salted water to the boil. Add your choice of pasta, such as spaghetti, and cook until al dente. Drain and divide between six bowls. Meanwhile, heat the sauce in a pan and add the cooked meatballs once it's simmering. Heat the meatballs until piping hot, then generously ladle the meatballs over the pasta. Finish with a sprinkling of nutritional yeast and more fresh basil.

Photo: Trevor Neal

I'm very fortunate to have travelled a lot over the years, with Pulp and otherwise, but even though I've seen about 65 countries now, there's nothing like coming home to Sheffield. The special nature of this city's people is always something to look forward to. You've got to see past the whole 'it's grim up north' stereotype; the greenery in Sheffield surprises people and opens their eyes. If I get asked whether I could live somewhere else, I have to honestly say not really because there's nowhere like it. Not many places have Hendo's to lash on your spag bol, at least!

NICK BANKS, DRUMMER

WELSH RAREBIT

PREPARATION TIME: 45 MINUTES IF MAKING CHEESE SAUCE, 5 MINUTES IF NOT | COOKING TIME: 5 MINUTES | SERVES: 6

FOR THE 'CHEESE' SAUCE

150g potato, peeled and cut into 1cm cubes

150g carrot, peeled and cut into 1cm slices

70g nutritional yeast

½ tsp smoked paprika

1 tsp garlic powder

1 tsp onion powder

2 tsp salt

3 tbsp lemon juice

150ml soy milk

FOR THE RAREBIT

200g cheese sauce, from above

50ml strong ale

1 tbsp wholegrain mustard

1 tsp distilled white vinegar

1 tsp cayenne pepper

1 tsp tamarind

Loaf of bread

Chives, chopped

FOR THE 'CHEESE' SAUCE

Steam or boil the potatoes and carrots until very soft (steaming means they won't absorb as much water so the consistency may be easier to manage).
Once cooked, allow the vegetables to cool and steam off slightly, then transfer into a large bowl and add 100ml of water along with all of the other ingredients. Using a stick blender, blitz everything together until the mixture is smooth and velvety. Add more water to thin the sauce out if needed, and more nutritional yeast to taste.

FOR THE RAREBIT

Whisk all the ingredients together except the chives. Cut two thick slices of bread per person. Generously spread the 'cheese' mixture onto each slice and place under the grill on a medium heat until golden and bubbly. Cover with chives and drown with Hendo's to serve.

Photo: Marco Borggreve

I'm still very attached to Sheffield. All my dad's family are from the city and I remember the old Henderson's factory as part of the fabric when I went to university there. My fondness for Hendo's has never left me either; I put it in lentil ragu, pasta sauces, stir fries…it's a great alternative to soy sauce especially for my twin toddlers who have certain allergies. Apart from Henderson's Relish, the hills are wonderful and the people are wonderful. I think they make the city; they are so warm-hearted.

ELIZABETH WATTS, OPERA SINGER

BAKED BEANS ON TOAST

PREPARATION TIME: 5 MINUTES | COOKING TIME: 30 MINUTES | SERVES: 4

2 cloves of garlic, finely minced
1 onion, finely minced
1 stick of celery, finely minced
1 carrot, finely minced
1 tbsp olive oil
2 tsp paprika
1 tbsp tomato purée
400g passata
60ml vegetable stock
300g tinned haricot beans
Salt and black pepper
Henderson's Relish

Most countries and regions have their own versions of this iconic dish, but interestingly, baked beans are hardly ever baked in an oven! This stove top recipe is super easy to prepare and made in just one pot. For smoky baked beans, simply replace the paprika with the smoked variety.

Sauté the garlic, onion, celery and carrot in the olive oil until soft and translucent. Add the paprika and tomato purée then cook for just a few seconds before pouring in the passata and stock. Bring to the boil then reduce to a simmer for 20 minutes. Add the tinned beans and cook out for a further 10 minutes. You know the beans are done when the sauce has thickened and is no longer sharp to taste. At this point you can adjust the seasoning with salt and black pepper.

TO SERVE

Cut and toast two slices of bread, lather with dairy-free spread and top with a generous helping of the beans. Throw on a couple dashes of Hendo's and tuck in.

I think Hendo's is a gift from Sheffield to the world. We're quite shy about trumpeting our successes here, but the time is right to push this wonderful product (especially for vegetarians and vegans – there's nothing fishy about this sauce!). I suppose I represent a landmark with Record Collector in the same way Henderson's does, so I care about being a promoter of Sheffield. My stance has always been to take a positive approach and tell people what's good about us. I still have a special edition Richard Hawley Hendo's bottle from his album launch at the old factory – there's a lot of pride in these things.

BARRY EVERARD, RECORD COLLECTOR

CHEESE DISHES

CHEESE AND ONION PIE

PREPARATION TIME: 2 HOURS | COOKING TIME: 40-60 MINUTES | SERVES: 4 (GENEROUS PORTIONS)

FOR THE SHORTCRUST PASTRY

500g plain flour
Salt and pepper
125g butter, diced
125g white vegetable fat, diced
125g egg, beaten

FOR THE FILLING

2 onions, diced
50g butter
1 tsp thyme leaves
500g mashed potato
200g mature cheddar, grated
¼ tsp grated nutmeg
Salt and pepper

FOR THE EGG WASH

2 egg yolks, beaten
1 tsp cold water
Pinch of salt

FOR THE SHORTCRUST PASTRY

Place the flour into a bowl and add a pinch of salt and pepper. Rub the diced butter and fat into the flour until the mixture resembles fine breadcrumbs.

Make a well in the centre of the mixture and gradually add the egg, combining everything with a table or palette knife as you go. Bring the pastry together then knead it gently until you have smooth dough. Flatten lightly and wrap in cling film. Place in the fridge for at least 30 minutes.

FOR THE FILLING

Sweat the onions in the butter until soft and golden then add the thyme. Combine the mash, cheese, onions and nutmeg in a large bowl. Season to taste with salt and pepper.

TO ASSEMBLE THE PIE

Line a 12cm springform tin with two thirds of the pastry, leaving an extra 2cm above the tin. Fill the pastry with the cheese and potato filling, adding a little extra butter and cheese on top if you like.

Roll out the last third of the pastry and cut out a 16cm circle for the pie lid. Egg wash the 2cm lip of the pastry case and place the lid over the filling. Seal the case and lid together, trim with scissors to leave a 1cm edge, then use your fingers to crimp the edge all the way around. Lightly score the lid with a sharp knife, whisk the egg wash ingredients together and brush them over all the exposed pastry, then chill the pie in the fridge for 30 minutes.

Egg wash the top of the pie again and then bake it at 180°c until the pastry is golden and crisp. Splash with Henderson's Relish before serving.

Photo: Lottie Davies

I first came to Sheffield in 1989 to study Psychology at the University. I knew as soon as I stepped off the train that this was where I was meant to be, and I've never left. The people here are unique; fiercely independent, proud and community driven. Never flashy or ostentatious, we would give away our last penny to help someone, but not pay a penny more than we need to when shopping for ourselves. I can't tell you how proud I am to be a member of parliament for this region; it truly is an honour to serve such decent folk.

SARAH CHAMPION, MP

CROQUE MONSIEUR

PREPARATION TIME: 5 MINUTES | COOKING TIME: 5 MINUTES | SERVES: 1

2 slices of good white bread
2 slices of cooked ham
Handful of grated cheddar cheese
Knob of butter

FOR THE BÉCHAMEL
50g butter
50g plain flour
300ml whole milk, warmed
Pinch of nutmeg, freshly grated

TO SERVE
Dijon mustard (optional)
Henderson's Relish

Butter the bread and place both slices butter side down on a board. Sprinkle the cheese over both pieces of bread then drizzle over as much Hendo's as you like. Place the ham on one side then sandwich the slices of bread together, butter side out, and press firmly.

Cook the toastie in a heavy-based frying pan until golden brown and crisp on both sides. Serve now or make it even more indulgent...

FOR THE BÉCHAMEL

There are many versions of this French classic, which might be baked, fried, covered with béchamel sauce or served with mustard mayonnaise.

To make your own béchamel sauce, first melt the butter in a small saucepan. Add the flour to the melted butter and mix to a smooth roux. Cook for a minute and then remove the pan from the heat. Add the warm milk gradually, making sure all the milk is incorporated before adding any more. You should have a smooth, silky, lump-free sauce. Stir in a pinch of freshly grated nutmeg to taste, if you like.

TO SERVE

Top the uppermost side of the toastie with béchamel sauce and place under a hot grill. Cook until bubbling and browned, then serve immediately with mustard, more Hendo's and your favourite side salad.

My oldest brother, my sister and I went to Sheffield for university but it's certainly true that the city became much more than a place we once studied in. I remember being particularly struck by the Henderson's Relish factory right in the centre, and the fact that you could smell it! We still have a strong connection with Sheffield, and for me what always stands out is how incredibly green and incredibly hilly it is. I also identify the place with driving along Snake Pass and football, which I spent nearly all my time playing during my undergrad degree.

SID LOWE, JOURNALIST AND WRITER

MAC 'N' CHEESE

PREPARATION TIME: 10 MINUTES | COOKING TIME: 10 MINUTES | SERVES: 4

300g macaroni
30g butter
25g flour
500ml milk
1 tsp mustard, or to taste
Salt and pepper, to taste
200g mature cheddar, grated

Preheat the oven to 180°c.

Cook the macaroni in a pan of boiling water until it's just underdone, draining it a couple of minutes earlier than you would usually. Retain a little bit of the cooking water.

While the macaroni is cooking, make the cheese sauce. Melt the butter in a medium-sized pan on a low heat. When the butter is foaming, add the flour and stir until it's mixed in. Continue cooking for 2 minutes, stirring frequently.

Very gradually add the milk, stirring constantly. Make sure each bit of milk is incorporated before adding the next bit. If you do this slowly on a very low heat, you should end up with a perfectly smooth sauce with no lumps and no need to whisk. However, if it does go wrong for some reason, you can always use a whisk to beat out the lumps.

When all the milk is incorporated, add the mustard, salt and pepper. Then add half the cheese, stir to combine and turn off the heat.

Tip the pasta and a couple of tablespoonfuls of the cooking water into the cheese sauce and stir until completely coated.

Pour the macaroni cheese into a shallow ovenproof dish and sprinkle over the remaining cheese. Bake in the preheated oven for 10 minutes until golden and bubbling, then serve with lashings of Henderson's Relish.

Photo: Paul Askew

I used to walk past the beautiful former Henderson's Relish factory every day on my way to university, and still use Hendo's in a lot of my cooking now. I love it with beans or cheese on toast, and as the secret ingredient in my son's favourite tomato pasta sauce recipe!

KATE JACKSON, ARTIST AND MUSICIAN

SOUTHERN FRIED HALLOUMI

225g halloumi

150ml milk

150g flour

1 tsp salt

1 tsp smoked paprika

¼ tsp cayenne

½ tsp white pepper

½ tsp garlic powder

½ tsp onion powder

FOR THE SALAD

200g mixed cherry tomatoes

100g plum tomatoes

2 medium vine tomatoes

1 small red onion, finely diced

1 clove of garlic, crushed

¼ tsp ground allspice

1 tsp white wine vinegar

1 tbsp pomegranate molasses

30ml olive oil

Salt and black pepper

1 pomegranate, deseeded

½ tbsp picked oregano leaves or finely sliced basil

First, cut the halloumi into batons and place them into the milk to soak.

Meanwhile, make your tomato, pomegranate and red onion salad. Halve the cherry tomatoes, dice the plum and vine tomatoes into small cubes then place all the tomatoes into a serving bowl with the diced red onion.

In a separate bowl, whisk the crushed garlic and allspice into the vinegar, pomegranate molasses and olive oil until combined. Add a little salt and black pepper to taste, then pour the dressing over the tomatoes.

Toss the tomatoes and onions in the dressing, then sprinkle over the pomegranate seeds and oregano or basil leaves. Set aside until the rest of the dish is ready. This refreshing combination provides a great contrast to the spiced and salty halloumi.

Combine the flour with the salt and all the spices, then remove the halloumi batons from the milk and toss them though the flour. To ensure they get an even coating, allow the halloumi to sit in the flour and toss two or three more times until a good layer has formed.

Remove the halloumi from the flour and deep fry at 180°c until golden and crisp. Drain on paper towels to remove excess oil, then serve immediately with the tomato, pomegranate and red onion salad.

When we ask our Sheffield Soup audience which ingredients should be in the quintessential recipe for the ultimate Sheffield Soup, time and again, the ingredient they insist upon is, of course, Hendo's. Henderson's Relish represents the taste and aroma of our great city, and – just like our project – is part of Sheffield's DNA.

PENNIE RAVEN, SHEFFIELD SOUP

TWICE BAKED
BLUE CHEESE SOUFFLÉ

PREPARATION TIME: 1 HOUR | COOKING TIME: 30 MINUTES | SERVES: 4

FOR THE BÉCHAMEL

50g butter, melted

50g plain flour

300ml whole milk, warmed

175g blue cheese, crumbled (or any other strong cheese)

1 tbsp Henderson's Relish

FOR THE SOUFFLÉ

Knob of butter, softened

2-3 tbsp plain flour

5 large eggs, separated

Salt and pepper

75g blue cheese (or any other strong cheese, as above)

50g butter

250ml cream

100g cheddar, grated

2 tbsp Henderson's Relish

Add spring onions, cherry tomatoes, chopped ham or diced peppers to the cream if you like

FOR THE BÉCHAMEL

Add the flour to the melted butter in a small saucepan and mix to a smooth roux. Cook for a minute and then remove the pan from the heat. Add the warm milk gradually, making sure all the milk is incorporated before adding any more. Then stir in the blue cheese until melted and add the Hendo's. Leave the pan off the heat while you make the soufflé.

FOR THE SOUFFLÉ

Preheat the oven to 220°c and half fill a roasting tin with hot water. Grease four 7.5cm by 4cm ramekins with butter, then dust with flour.

Whisk the egg yolks into the béchamel, then whisk the egg whites separately until they form stiff peaks. Stir one third of the whites into the béchamel and mix well. Gently fold in the remaining whites using a metal spoon, taking care not to knock the air out.

Fill each ramekin with the béchamel to just below the rim. Gently push a piece of the blue cheese into each one. Place the ramekins in the roasting tin and cook for about 15 to 20 minutes in the oven. They should rise to twice their original height and turn golden on top.

Carefully remove the ramekins from the tin then turn out the soufflés onto a cooling rack or plate. They will deflate while cooling.

Grease a dish with butter and place the soufflés in. Drizzle with a little cream and add a few knobs of butter, sprinkle the cheese and some Henderson's over each soufflé then bake in the oven for about 12 minutes until golden and risen slightly.

Serve with a green salad and crusty bread or as a starter.

At Sheffield College we provide training and education to hundreds of trainee chefs and front of house staff. Alongside Henderson's Relish, the Sheffield College Catering department is an institution in Sheffield, both having a strong following. Where recipes call for the 'unmentionable' of the sauces we always turn to Hendo's instead! Whether in our own Silver Plate Restaurant or nationwide competitions, we are never too far away from a bottle.

CHEF TUTORS AT SHEFFIELD COLLEGE

TASTY SIDES

ROAST POTATOES

PREPARATION TIME: 10 MINUTES | COOKING TIME: 1 HOUR | SERVES: 4

1kg Maris Piper potato
100g duck or goose fat or 100ml olive oil
Sea salt, to serve

Put a roasting tin in the oven (one big enough to take the potatoes in a single layer) and heat the oven to 200°c (180°c).

Peel the potatoes and cut each one into three or four evenly sized pieces so they are about 5cm cubes. Place the potatoes into a large pan and pour in enough water to barely cover them. Add salt, turn on the heat then wait for the water to boil. As soon as the water reaches a full rolling boil, lower the heat, put your timer on and simmer the potatoes, uncovered, for 2 minutes.

Put the duck or goose fat or olive oil into the hot roasting tin and heat in the oven for a few minutes. Drain the potatoes in a colander then shake the colander back and forth a few times to fluff up the outsides. Carefully put the potatoes into the hot fat, then turn and roll them around so they are coated all over. Spread them out in a single layer, making sure they have plenty of room.

Roast the potatoes in the oven for 15 minutes, then take them out of the oven and turn them over.

Roast for another 15 minutes and turn them over again. Put them back in the oven for another 10 to 20 minutes until golden and crisp. Season with sea salt and serve straight away.

MUSHY PEAS

PREPARATION TIME: 5 MINUTES | COOKING TIME: 30-45 MINUTES, PLUS 12 HOURS SOAKING | SERVES: 4

225g dried marrowfat peas
2 tbsp baking soda
Salt and pepper, to taste

Place the peas in a large bowl or stockpot; the peas will swell and need plenty of room to expand. Add the baking soda, cover with 285ml boiling water and stir to make sure the baking soda has dissolved. Leave the peas to soak overnight or for a minimum of 12 hours.

Drain the peas in a colander, and then place them in a large saucepan. Cover them with cold water and bring this to the boil. Lower the heat and simmer for approximately 30 minutes or until the peas have softened and turned mushy.

Season with salt and pepper and splash on plenty of Henderson's Relish.

FOCACCIA WITH ROSEMARY AND SEA SALT

PREPARATION TIME: 1 HOUR 45 MINUTES | COOKING TIME: 30 MINUTES | SERVES: 6

15g fresh yeast
350ml water
500g strong white flour
1 ½ tsp salt
3 tbsp olive oil
Dried rosemary
Course rock salt

Add the yeast to approximately half of the water, and stir to dissolve it. Mix the flour and salt together in a large bowl. Make a well in the centre and pour in the yeasted water and one tablespoon of the olive oil. Stir the liquid into the flour and then gradually add the remaining water to form a soft, sticky dough. Use more water if necessary.

Turn the dough out onto a clean surface and knead until smooth, silky and elastic. This should take about 10 minutes. Put the dough into an oiled bowl and cover. Leave to prove until doubled in size.

Knock back the dough gently and turn out onto a lightly floured work surface. Stretch the dough with your hands until you have a large round. Using your fingertips, make lots of indentations in the dough and then drizzle it with the remaining olive oil. Scatter over the rosemary and rock salt and leave the focaccia to prove for another 10 to 20 minutes.

Bake in a preheated oven at 200°c for approximately 25 minutes or until golden. Remove the focaccia from the oven and transfer to a wire rack to cool for 30 minutes or so, before ripping the bread apart and serving with your favourite Italian meal.

HENDO'S BUTTER

PREPARATION TIME: 5 MINUTES | SERVES: 6-8

250g salted butter
1 bottle of Henderson's Relish

Place the softened butter into a mixer, add approximately one quarter of the Hendo's and beat the butter until all the Hendo's has been incorporated. Add more Hendo's for a darker colour and stronger flavour if you wish.

STUFFED JACKET POTATOES

PREPARATION TIME: 10 MINUTES | COOKING TIME: 40 MINUTES | SERVES: 4

4 medium fluffy potatoes
(approximately 350g), such as Maris
Piper or King Edward

100ml soured cream

2 tbsp double cream

3 tbsp chives, finely chopped

Salt and pepper

100g butter, melted

Preheat the oven to 180°c. Season the potatoes then place them on the top shelf of the oven for 30 to 40 minutes until the skin is crisp and the flesh is soft.

Remove the potatoes from the oven. Halve them and scoop out most of the flesh. Roughly mash the flesh in a bowl with the soured cream, cream and chives. Season the mixture and spoon it back into the potato skins.

Brush them with melted butter, then return the potatoes to the oven and bake for a further 15 minutes until golden. Top with Henderson's Relish.

MASHED POTATO

PREPARATION TIME: 10 MINUTES | COOKING TIME: 15-20 MINUTES | SERVES: 4-6

1kg floury potatoes (such as King Edward or Maris Piper)

100ml double cream

150g butter

Salt and pepper

Bring a large saucepan of water to the boil while you peel and chop the potatoes into evenly sized pieces. Put the potatoes into the pan and boil for about 15 minutes, or until tender. Transfer to a colander and drain well, then place back in the pan off the heat.

Heat the cream and butter in a small pan, then pour over the potatoes. Mash the potatoes using an electric hand whisk or potato masher until smooth and free from lumps. Season with pepper and a pinch of salt.

BRAISED RED CABBAGE

PREPARATION TIME: 10 MINUTES | COOKING TIME: APPROX. 30 MINUTES | SERVES: 4 (AS A SIDE)

1 small red cabbage
100g butter
1 tbsp ground allspice
1 tbsp Demerara sugar
Salt and pepper
150ml cider vinegar

Finely slice the red cabbage and place it into a saucepan with the butter. Scatter over the spice, sugar, salt and pepper.

Place on a medium heat and add the vinegar. Bring to the boil then reduce the heat to a simmer, cover and cook for 25 to 30 minutes, stirring regularly, until the cabbage is cooked through.

When the cabbage is cooked through, drain in a colander and then place in a serving dish.

The cabbage can be made ahead of time and reheated in a covered dish in the oven or microwave until piping hot.

GLAZED CARROTS

PREPARATION TIME: 5 MINUTES | COOKING TIME: 10-20 MINUTES | SERVES: 2

1 large carrot or 6 baby carrots
50g butter
30g caster sugar
Pinch of salt

Peel the large carrot or wash the baby carrots, then cut into attractive shapes. Place in a saucepan with enough water to just cover them and add the butter, sugar and salt.

Bring to the boil and cook until the carrots are tender and the liquid has reduced to a glaze. If there is still a lot of liquid left, remove the carrots and keep reducing, then return the carrots to the pan to heat through before serving.

Check the seasoning and finish the carrots in the oven for extra colour if you like.

Photo: Paul Cocker

INDEX

HENDERSON'S RELISH

For Chops, Steaks, Soups, Fish & Game

Ingredients: Water, Sugar, Malt Vinegar, Colour
Caramel, Syrup, Salt, Tamarinds, Acetic Acid,
Cayenne Pepper, Cloves, Saccharin, Garlic Oil,
Emulsifier, E413 (or Tragacanth), ISO propyl alcohol.

SHAKE THE BOTTLE

HENDERSONS (Sheffield) LTD.
Leavygreave Road, Sheffield S3 7RA

284 ml
10 Fl. Ozs

BEST BEFORE END
SEPT 1995

L 2303

5 021016 990999

HENDERSON'S
RELISH

SHAKE THE
BOTTLE

LARG
END
R

SHAKE T

HENDERSON

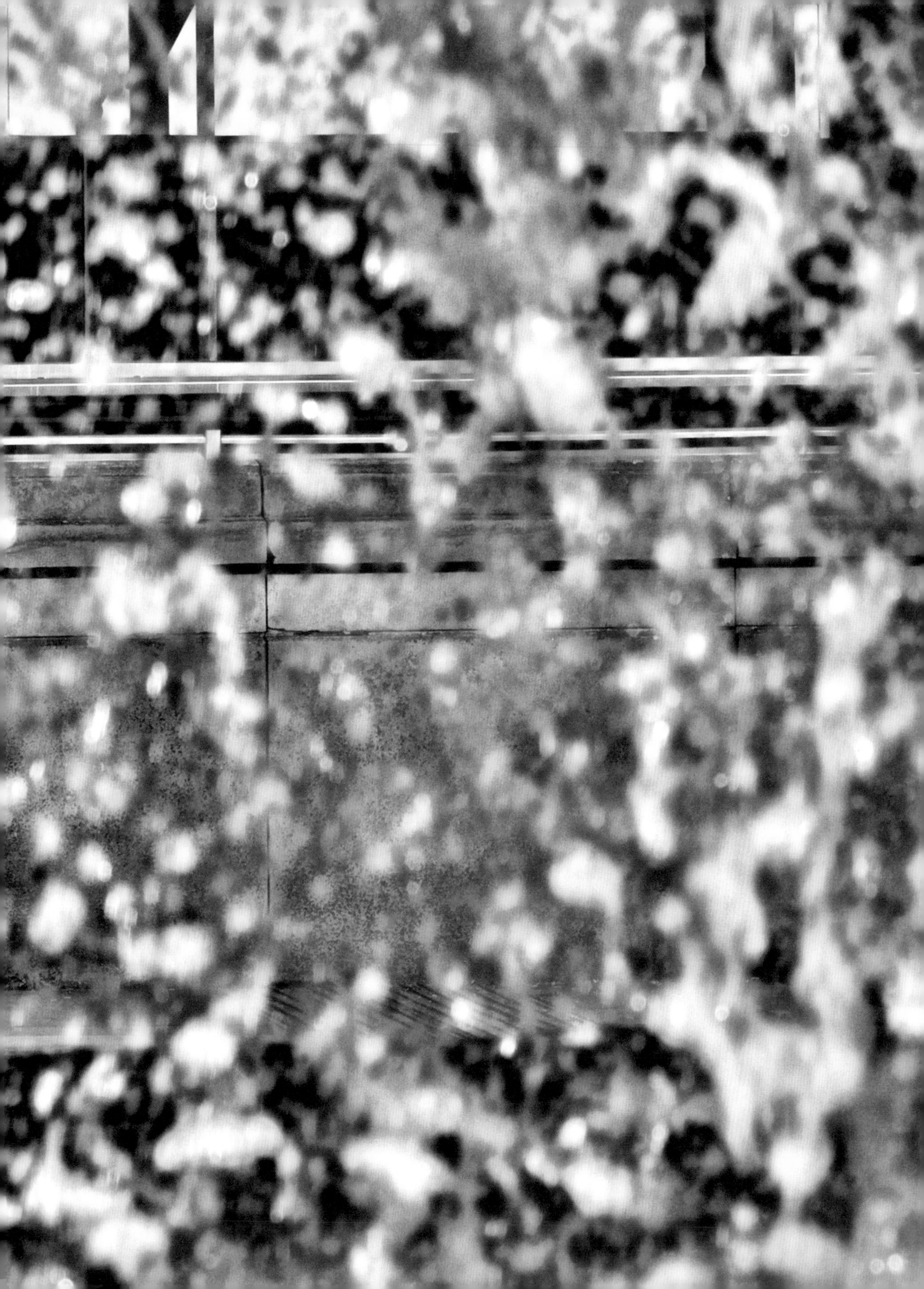

We would like to thank Gregg Rodgers, Andy Gabbitas,
Neil Taylor, Joseph Hunt from Sheffield College and
Adam Clark (not pictured) from Make No Bones
for putting all of the recipes together.